THE URBAN HOUSE

THE URBAN HOUSE

TOWNHOUSES, APARTMENTS, LOFTS, AND OTHER SPACES FOR CITY LIVING

RON BROADHURST
FOREWORD
BY RICHARD MEIER

RIZZOLI
NEW YORK

New York · Paris · London · Milan

First published in the United States of America in 2014
by Rizzoli International Publications, Inc.
300 Park Avenue South
New York, NY 10010
www.rizzoliusa.com

2014 2015 2016 2017 / 10 9 8 7 6 5 4 3 2 1

Distributed in the U.S. trade by Random House, New York

Design by Claudia Brandenburg, Language Arts

Printed in China

ISBN-13: 978-0-8478-3955-1

Library of Congress Control Number: 2013950440

THE URBAN HOUSE
FOREWORD
BY RICHARD MEIER

At the beginning of my career as an architect I lived in a two-room apartment in a brownstone building on East 91st Street. There I slept in one room and worked in the other. Reflecting upon all of that now I look back and think of how things have changed and how New York City, and the architecture of the city, has gone through numerous changes.

Since the beginning of the twentieth century, there has been a tremendous physical growth of urban areas. Modern architecture developed and since then it has continued to be the foundation for architecture and design. *The Urban House* is a distinctive and careful selection of private residences located in city centers in the United States, Europe, and Australia. All of these urban interventions reflect very unique and particular solutions to all the different locations. The architecture in all these spaces reflects nature, and interacts with nature, and they all deal with the quality of light, program, and human scale.

When I look outside the window of my office in Manhattan, the light changes, the sky changes, the color changes, and the weather changes. Modern architecture should allow us to appreciate all the changes that occur in nature, and there needs to be an interaction between the interior and exterior space. The light in New York is very different from the light in Barcelona, and in the projects compiled in *The Urban House* one can appreciate how the architects and designers have manipulated the orientation of the space, the context, and the quality of light to create compelling and interesting residential spaces.

The projects in this book reflect a very diverse portfolio of work and different attitudes toward architecture. It reflects unique ideas of what architecture could be, and particular orders and styles that contribute to the discourse of modern architecture in cities around the world.

INTRODUCTION
RON BROADHURST

Very recently cities have become home to most of the world's population. The tipping point came in 2010, when more than half the population lived in urban areas, compared with, for instance, less than 40 percent in 1990, according to the World Health Organization. And the figure will have more than doubled between 2009, when 2.5 billion people lived in cities, and 2050, when more than 5 billion will be urban dwellers. Such rapid growth is to take place largely in developing countries; still, in high-income countries—where the projects composing this book are located—urban population levels will remain stable over the next two decades. And of these urban dwellers, half live in cities with populations between 100,000 and 500,000, as opposed to 10 percent who live in so-called megacities, such as London or New York. The projects featured here reflect this fact, with not only New York, London, Los Angeles, Sydney, Chicago, and Barcelona represented but also Washington, D.C., Rotterdam, Dublin, Ghent, and San Sebastián, Spain.

Among these projects, the Brooklyn Brownstone, designed by Juergen Riehm of the firm 1100 Architect, most closely adheres to the classic urban ideal: Riehm undertook its renovation in such a manner as to retain and rejuvenate the gracious spaces that comprised the original Gothic Revival townhouse while completely refashioning an ill-conceived two-story addition at the rear of the house into a sleek aluminum-and-glass pavilion. Like the townhouse, the loft has come to embody an ideal for urban spaces updated for contemporary living, and is here most classically represented by UNStudio's Art Collector's Loft. However, the firm's principals, Ben van Berkel and Caroline Bos, have introduced their inimitable fluid, pristine forms to make an iconic twentieth-century residential type into an innovative signature project.

Three additional Manhattan residences represent an even more refined ideal of urban living: the gracious prewar high-rise apartment. However, architects Thomas Phifer and Richard Meier transformed the respective apartments they designed—with each of the two apartments coincidentally overlooking Central Park from high above Fifth Avenue—from a series of small, discrete spaces better suited to the formalities of early-twentieth-century life into spatially fluid, light-filled aeries. Yet despite the remarkable similarities between the two apartments' programs, each has highly distinctive profiles, with the apartment designed by Meier warmed by honey-colored wood paneling, details, and built-in bookcases, while the apartment designed by Phifer serves as a sort of highly polished gallery optimized for showcasing the client's collection of Minimalist art and classic modernist furniture. Conversely, on the other side of the park, in the landmark Beresford building on the Upper West Side, the guiding principle for architects Mark Ferguson and Oscar Shamamian was restraint, allowing the streamlined grandeur of the unique five-story apartment to speak for itself.

That these archetypal urban residences are in Manhattan or Brooklyn points to the fact that New York City is the locale for more than half of the projects comprising this volume. But among the remaining projects located in New York City that are featured here there is considerable variety in design approaches. Just as the Upper East Side apartments designed by Meier and Phifer are so distinct from one another despite their similar types and programs, the architects behind the other nine New York residences have brought to bear their own strong aesthetic sensibilities to arrive at as many distinct approaches to a surprising variety of residential types.

Take for example the firm 1100 Architect, whose work is represented here not only by the Brooklyn Brownstone but also by a project in lower Manhattan, the Harrison Street Residence. Where the former project is a marriage between a graceful nineteenth-century domestic structure and a light-filled, function-oriented addition, the Harrison Street Residence radically recasts an unremarkable commercial building dating from 1919 to become a structure as distinguished by its rational planning as for the refinement of its details and transforming the original dowager warehouse building into a glamorous palazzo. Now consider the house for conceptual artist Lawrence Weiner designed by LOT-EK, headed by Ada Tolla and Giuseppe Lignano. Also located in lower Manhattan and of similar scale to the Harrison Street Residence, the Weiner Townhouse could not have less in common with the Harrison Street Residence from a design perspective, with Tolla and Lignano's signature use of repurposed industrial materials in full effect, from exposed electrical conduits to recycled shipping containers.

The bold use of industrial materials including Cor-ten steel panels and polished concrete floors can also be found in Dean/Wolf Architects' Inverted Warehouse/Townhouse, a sprawling residence occupying the upper five floors of a narrow six-story warehouse building in TriBeCa. But here what immediately impresses is the scale of the residence, as well as the complexity of its myriad interlocking indoor and outdoor spaces, making it one of a TriBeCa-based triad of "megalofts" featured in this volume, each designed to satisfy the functions of real life as well as those of large-scale entertaining. The NYC Loft, designed by Allied Works Architecture, is perhaps the sleekest of the three, thanks to firm principle Brad Cloepfil's integration of such rough-hewn materials as cast aluminum and concrete with the refinement of white marble and warm mahogany. And the White Street Loft, designed by Work Architecture Company, is undoubtedly the most playful of the three, with structural details of the nineteenth-century cast-iron warehouse space serving as the foundation for a kaleidoscope of materials, circulation systems, and spatial arrangements.

The virtual antithesis of these megalofts in industrial spaces is probably best represented by the Charles Street Townhouse, designed by Messana O'Rorke, in Manhattan's West Village, and its Georgetown counterpart, the house Washington, D.C.–based architect Simon Jacobsen designed for himself. Occupying structures that date from the mid-nineteenth century within a decade of one another and fronting their respective streets with unusually wide facades, each of these houses represents the transformation of appealingly homely structures into ingeniously reconfigured spaces that offer copious light and state-of-the-art amenities while respecting the integrity of the original structures.

The house in Brooklyn designed by David Adjaye is as alien to its context as the Charles Street and Georgetown townhouses are deferential to theirs. A wholly new construction, the Pitch Black House is expressive not only of its function as a living and studio space for a pair of artists but also of Adjaye's masterful, even sculptural, minimalist aesthetic. Adjaye shares the mantle of minimalist master with John Pawson, whose Old Town Apartment in Ghent, Belgium, is as serenely austere as the monasteries and churches he has designed in the Czech Republic, Hungary, and Germany. With Pawson and Richard Meier, Andrée Putman completes a triumvirate of designers featured in these pages whose careers are emblematic of the high modernism of the late twentieth century. Her death in 2012 represents the abrupt close of a chapter of modernist history that encompassed the reintroduction of early-twentieth-century modern furniture through her company Écart, the design of the first so-called boutique hotel, Morgans in New York, and the redesign of the interior of the iconic Concorde for Air France.

The preeminence achieved by Putman in the field of design could be considered a pioneering role validated by the fact that of the twenty-five projects presented in this volume, eleven are the product of female designers or firms headed by women. One hopes that number demonstrates a trend toward parity in the twenty-first century for a profession dominated by men more pervasively than most. Perhaps the most closely aligned inheritor of Putman's legacy among the architects featured in these pages is Annabelle Selldorf, noted as she is for designing such prominent cultural institutions as the Neue Galerie Museum for German and Austrian Art, in New York, with a comprehensive eye toward giving equal due to existing contextual elements as well as new formal interventions. This subtle approach is perfectly demonstrated in the East Village Townhouse, which Selldorf designed for two art collectors. Here Selldorf introduced open, light-filled spaces while retaining a strong sense of the presence of the original nineteenth-century structure. With another project included here, also in New York, the Chelsea Loft, Selldorf took a freer hand, naturally, with a residence that occupies part of a former YMCA gymnasium. A similarly unbridled approach characterizes the design for the Brick Weave House by Studio Gang Architects, headed by Jeanne Gang. For this Chicago house Gang radically reconceived a fire-damaged structure into a slick sequence of gallery-like spaces fronted by a virtuosic double-height filigreed brick wall.

The formal wit on display in the brick weave of the Brick Weave House is shared with Barbara Bestor's Floating Bungalow, in the Los Angeles neighborhood of Venice. Here Bestor conceived of the project as a second-story, white, bungalow-shaped "cloud" floating over a ground level concealed by its dark charcoal color. Some may consider Los Angeles to be pushing the definition of "urban" too far. But with the population density of Los Angeles overall nearing that of London, and the location of the Floating Bungalow in one of the city's more densely populated enclaves, its inclusion should not be surprising, nor should the fact that the other Los Angeles house featured here is also to be found in Venice. The Vertical House, which architect Lorcan O'Herlihy designed for himself, derives its name and its concept from its dense context. Here the site required O'Herlihy to adhere to a narrow footprint and stack the house's living spaces around a central stair core.

Both Bestor and O'Herlihy are closely identified with their home city, with Bestor having generated a portfolio of residences for Los Angeles's creative elite and O'Herlihy consistently exploring ways to bring sustainable design to Angeleno urban life. But the commission for the Flynn Mews House, in Dublin, gave O'Herlihy the irresistible opportunity to build in his native Ireland for the first time. That the commission also involved adhering to a building code requiring the preservation of elements of a nineteenth-century neoclassical carriage house, as well as a clearly modernist cast to any new construction, brought a unique set of challenges. The result is a radically ingenious intervention in the service of preserving a fragment of history. A similar act of architectural sleight of hand is at work in Chenchow Little's Skylight House, in Sydney, where an intricately louvered and sculpted ceiling is concealed behind a meticulously restored Victorian facade.

In Rotterdam, Rolf Bruggink took the contrary approach with the house he built for himself and called simply the Black Pearl. Here the whole-cloth reconfiguration of the interior spaces bursts through the pitch-black-painted facade in the form of metal-framed apertures that pierce the covered-over formwork of the original sash windows. A similarly irreverent approach was adopted by architect Sally Mackereth for the Little Venice House, in London, where two nineteenth-century structures—a carriage house and workshop—have been radically transformed into the ultimate bachelor pad where the most antique-looking elements are in fact newly crafted. In the Crusch Alba Loft, on the other hand, architect Gus Wüstemann has designed the free-flowing sequence of living spaces to act as a series of palimpsests that reveal multiple layers of structural elements and decorative finishes. In this residence, which Wüstemann designed for himself and his family, the architect has balanced openness and fluidity with flexible spatial divisions, so that in a nineteenth-century apartment house in Barcelona's oldest quarter, a classically open-spaced loft is born out of the most traditional of urban structures.

THE URBAN

TOWNHOUSES, AP
AND OTHER SPACE

HOUSE
ARTMENTS, LOFTS,
S FOR CITY LIVING

1100 ARCHITECT
HARRISON STREET RESIDENCE
NEW YORK, NEW YORK

The neighborhood of TriBeCa in lower Manhattan has experienced a series of transformations over the course of the twentieth century that has taken it from a center of commerce to an artists' haven to one of the city's most expensive residential neighborhoods. Taking its name from the abbreviation for "Triangle Below Canal Street," TriBeCa had been colonized by artists during the 1970s following the decline of the area's industry, which left unoccupied expansive commercial space available at relatively low cost. Beginning in the 1980s, TriBeCa began to experience steady gentrification and now, along with the Upper East Side and the West Village, commands the highest prices per square foot in the city. The architecture firm 1100 Architect, headed by David Piscuskas and Juergen Riehm and based in New York and Frankfurt, proved to be the ideal choice to take on this commission to convert a relatively small-scale commercial building dating from 1919 into a generous three-level residence perfectly suited for twenty-first-century living.

Since its founding in 1983, the firm has generated a portfolio of projects that balances refined residential commissions with cultural and educational projects that include buildings for New York University and Columbia University Medical Center, and public library projects in Queens, the Bronx, and Battery Park City, in lower Manhattan. Among their early projects was the reconstruction of the 12,500-square-foot, two-story warehouse belonging to Pop artist Roy Lichtenstein, who used it as his studio and residence. So it was with considerable experience negotiating the built context and cultural landscape of New York City that the architects approached this project, first restoring the building's exterior cladding of glazed terra-cotta panels to meet the exacting standards of the city's Landmarks Preservation Commission. Other than reserving the building's ground level as commercial space, the architects were free to rebuild its upper two levels, to which they added a rooftop-level addition and terrace.

The first level of the residence accommodates a long, open space comprising the living space, dining space, and kitchen. The north- and east-facing walls are entirely given over to the large-scale warehouse windows typical of commercial structures of this era in the city, flooding the space with natural light, while the length of the dining area on the wall opposite the windows is composed of rich wooden panels that conceal storage space. The second level contains the master bedroom suite as well as a second bedroom and bath, all extremely generously proportioned. At the rooftop level, the architects introduced a newly constructed pavilion that serves as an expansive wood-paneled den and that features an undulating floor-to-ceiling glass wall overlooking the limestone-tiled rooftop terrace. The series of staircases linking the three levels is exquisitely detailed with recessed handrails and, between the second level and the rooftop pavilion, translucent treads and a sculptural bronze latticed partition.

1100 Architect converted a relatively small-scale commercial building dating from 1919 into a generous three-level residence, including the addition of a glass-enclosed rooftop pavilion.

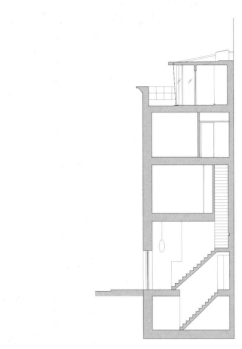

CROSS SECTION

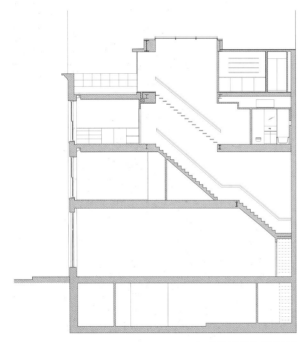

LONGITUDINAL SECTION

The first level of the residence accommodates a long, open space comprising the living space, dining space, and kitchen, with north- and east-facing walls entirely given over to the large-scale warehouse windows, flooding the space with natural light.

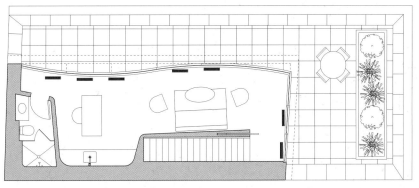

THIRD FLOOR PLAN

The length of the
dining area on the wall
opposite the windows
is composed of rich
wooden panels that
conceal storage space.

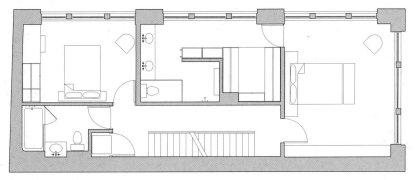

SECOND FLOOR PLAN

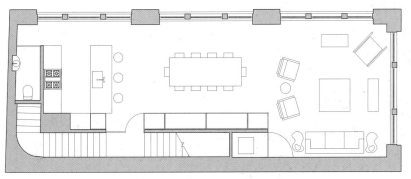

FIRST FLOOR PLAN

Left: A series of stair-cases links the house's three living levels and features exquisitely detailed, sculptural recessed handrails. Opposite: A view from the master bedroom to its spacious en suite bathroom.

Opposite, top and bottom: The staircase between the second level and the rooftop pavilion features translucent treads and a sculptural bronze latticed partition.
Left: The rooftop addition contains a den and office, accessing a spacious limestone-tiled terrace.

23

The rooftop pavilion's undulating floor-to-ceiling glass wall is modulated by the dark wood-paneled wall opposite.

Architect Lorcan O'Herlihy designed this house as his own residence in the beachside Venice neighborhood of Los Angeles, where houses are typically in extremely close proximity to one another. The house's structural skin of standardized precast concrete panels offered O'Herlihy the flexibility to punctuate the house's surfaces with nearly one hundred windows.

LORCAN O'HERLIHY ARCHITECTS
VERTICAL HOUSE
VENICE, CALIFORNIA

Though it is usually associated with archetypal suburban sprawl, and justifiably so, Los Angeles also maintains within its boundaries densely populated pockets developed organically over the past century or more. One such enclave is Venice, the beachside neighborhood that was originally conceived during the first decade of the twentieth century as a master-planned vacation community, and which now sustains a population density of approximately 12,000 per square mile, on a par with that of London, at around 13,500 per square mile. Houses typically are in extremely close proximity to one another, and this house, designed by architect Lorcan O'Herlihy as his own residence, is no exception. Irish-born O'Herlihy gained experience as a young architect working on such iconic cultural projects as Kevin Roche and John Dinkeloo's hall for the Temple of Dendur at the Metropolitan Museum of Art and I. M. Pei's project for the Louvre, after which he established his own practice in Los Angeles dedicated to an innovative use of materials as well as explorations into sustainable design.

For his own house on a typically narrow Venice site, O'Herlihy conceived of a towerlike 2,400-square-foot structure with a simple layout organized around a central stair core. At the ground level the entry to the structure is an unpretentious progression from carport to studio, with a staircase accessing the first main level, which accommodates the house's two bedrooms. One level up, on the house's highest full floor, O'Herlihy has placed the living and dining rooms to take advantage of views of the Pacific Ocean. A simple, single-counter kitchen occupies one wall of the dining space. At the rear of the house an outdoor spiral staircase links all three levels. Crowning the structure is a rooftop terrace with a micropavilion composed entirely of what is effectively a standalone window seat.

The house's steel structural frame permits a high degree of formal flexibility for the structural skin of standardized precast concrete panels. O'Herlihy capitalized on this flexibility to maximum effect by punctuating the house's surfaces with nearly one hundred windows that are either transparent, translucent, or colored. Some of the windows extend between floor plates so that a window placed toward the ceiling of the second level may appear peeking up from the floor of the third level. The variations in transparency and array of colors give the boxlike volume of the house an unexpected and satisfying texture and complexity.

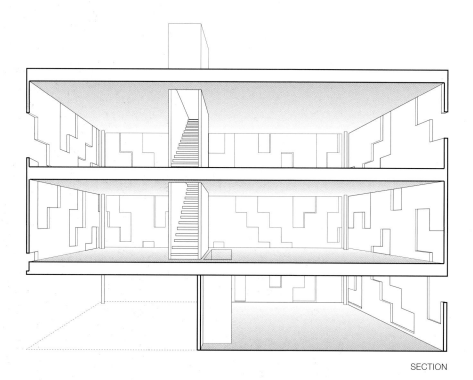

SECTION

The house's many windows are either transparent, translucent, or colored, with some windows extending between floor plates so that a window placed toward the ceiling of the second level may appear peeking up from the floor of the third level.

The main living level is placed on the top floor to maximize views, and is given over to a dining space, one wall of which is occupied by a single-counter kitchen, and beyond that the internal stair volume and the main living space, which accesses an outdoor spiral staircase that links all three levels of the house.

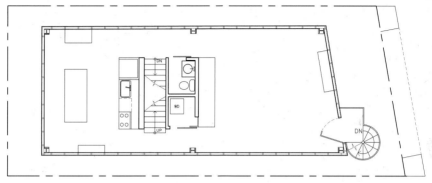

THIRD FLOOR PLAN

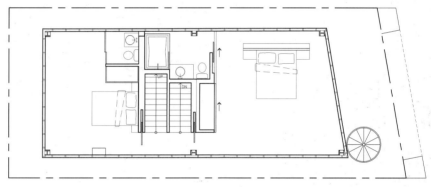

SECOND FLOOR PLAN

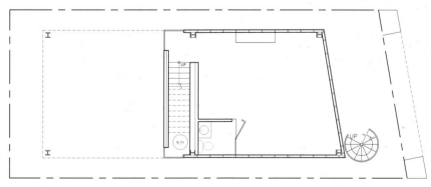

FIRST FLOOR PLAN

The living room and bedrooms feature multicolored wood-paneled built-in storage spaces that complement the kaleidoscope effect of the variety of windows.

Left: The Vertical House derives its name from O'Herlihy's conception of a towerlike 2,400-square-foot structure with a simple layout organized around a central stair core.
Opposite: The house is crowned by a rooftop terrace with a micropavilion composed entirely of what is effectively a standalone window seat.

ANDRÉE PUTMAN
SAN SEBASTIÁN APARTMENT
SAN SEBASTIÁN, SPAIN

Before her death in 2012, Andrée Putman was already a national treasure in her native France and a seminal figure in the history of modernist design thanks not only to her own iconic projects but also to her earlier work reviving classic modernist furniture pieces through her company Écart. Though she was considered a maverick, even eccentric, when she began her design career during the 1970s, over time her work has maintained a timelessness that makes it difficult to date. This lasting quality emerges in large part from her pared-down, almost minimalist approach to design, an approach that struck the popular consciousness with her interiors for the Morgans Hotel, the first "boutique hotel," and continued with such notable commissions as a redesign of the cabin of Air France's legendary Concorde and interiors for the French ministries of culture and education.

In San Sebastián, a beachside city on the northern coast of Spain's Basque country that sits at the mouth of the Urumea River, Putman designed a penthouse apartment with an expansive terrace overlooking the river. Though it is a small city, San Sebastián features a dense central district built during the late nineteenth and early twentieth centuries in the Haussmannian style, complete with a train station designed in part by Gustave Eiffel. This is where Putman combined three separate studio apartments to create a sprawling two-bedroom residence where dramatic circulation dominates the plan.

One enters into a long corridor that extends from the kitchen and dining room at one end of the apartment past a series of French doors that open onto the large terrace and terminates at a small study. The corridor itself maintains the dimensions of a considerable room, though one dedicated to the provision of views, copious natural light, and an organizational spine from which the entire apartment radiates. The openness created by this corridor is modulated by sliding partitions designed by Putman, constructed of wood frames with fabric panels. These panels separate the dining room from the warm and sun-filled kitchen as well as allow the study to become a discrete room by separating it from the large corridor. Sculptural hanging bookshelves distinguish the study from a surprisingly intimately scaled living room that is arranged around a large, circular light well clad entirely in translucent glass blocks. The living room is flanked on either end by doors to the apartment's two bedrooms, one a modestly scaled guest bedroom with an ingeniously compact shower room, and the other a master bedroom whose scale counters the comparatively diminutive living room. In the master bedroom Putman created a room within a room in the form of a sleeping alcove paneled entirely in Macassar ebony. The flow of spaces that compose this sequence terminates in the extravagantly proportioned master bathroom, which is clad in blue and white tiles in a myriad of shapes and tones, and features Putman's trademark ball-footed bathtub.

In San Sebastián, a beachside city on the northern coast of Spain's Basque country that sits at the mouth of the Urumea River, this penthouse apartment features an expansive terrace overlooking the river.

The intimately scaled living room is arranged around a large, circular light well clad entirely in translucent glass blocks. Just beyond this light well, hanging bookshelves separate the living room from the study.

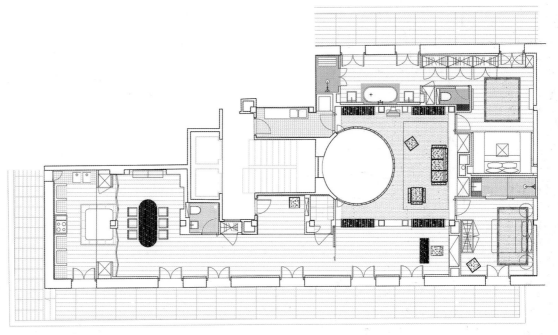

PLAN

Left: Just to the left
of the custom-designed
hanging bookshelves,
the study opens to the
living room.
Top right: The study
is the termination
point at one end of the
expansive entrance
corridor and can be
cordoned off by sliding
partitions designed
by Putman.
Bottom right: The
guest bedroom features
an ingeniously compact
shower room.

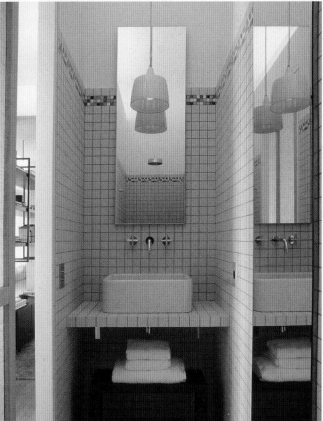

Left: The small study features a built-in fold-down desk with drawers and cabinets concealed behind custom-designed panels. Opposite: The other end of the entrance corridor terminates at the kitchen and dining room.

Opposite: The kitchen is also easily concealed behind custom-designed partitions, though folding rather than sliding as in the study.
Left: White cabinetry, tile work, and marble countertops contribute a sense of lightness to the already sun-filled kitchen.

Wood accents under the oversized kitchen island (left) and the custom-designed wood table and Thonet seating in the dining room (opposite) add warmth to the adjacent rooms.

Left: The spacious
master bathroom fea-
tures intricate tile work
as well as Putman's
trademark ball-footed
bathtub.
Opposite: In the master
bedroom Putman
created a room within
a room in the form
of a sleeping alcove
paneled entirely in
Macassar ebony.

DAVID ADJAYE
PITCH BLACK HOUSE
BROOKLYN, NEW YORK

London-based architect David Adjaye has gained worldwide fame as a designer of Spartan exhibition spaces—including the Rivington Place arts complex in London, the Museum of Contemporary Art in Denver, and the National Museum of African American History and Culture in Washington DC—with a tendency to emphasize the sculptural possibilities inherent in the meticulous manipulation of natural light. In these sleek spaces a minimum of illumination goes a long way. His numerous house designs similarly rely on the formal qualities of light to create living spaces that favor a sense of formal edginess over domestic comfort. With the Pitch Black House, commissioned by a pair of artists, Adjaye found himself constructing an enigmatic structure appearing as a matte-black monolith from the street front, while its rear facade is composed largely of wood-framed glass panels.

The house was built on the site of a carriage house adjacent to a church and rectory on one side and a parking lot on the other, in a socially diverse Brooklyn neighborhood. Its front facade derives its impenetrable profile from a cladding of black polypropylene panels, and is actually the first of two facades, between which light wells extending the full height of the structure provide both maximum privacy and diffuse illumination. Living spaces are arranged over three floors, while each of two studios occupies its own floor, one at ground level and one at attic level. Indeed Adjaye has given pride of place to both artists' spaces, which feature double-height studios and separate offices.

The complexity of the double facade and the strategic placement of the studio spaces at the bottom and top of the building create the potential for a dramatic promenade sequence throughout the house's interior spaces. Adjaye capitalizes on this potential with multiple staircases—some concealed, some in full view, and all detailed with exquisitely formed concrete handrails illuminated with hidden fluorescent light—beginning with the stair from the ground level, which is tucked into a niche and leads to the mezzanine office overlooking the ground-floor studio. A hairpin turn leads to another staircase, up to the third level, where the main living spaces of the house are located. Here the expansive open space accommodating living room, dining room, and kitchen is modulated by elements such as a discreetly placed powder room and multiple wooden built-ins including bookshelves, cabinets, and a settee.

Commissioned by a pair of artists, the Pitch Black House features an array of refined details, such as the built-in wooden bookshelves, cabinets, and settee in the main living space.

The front facade of
the Pitch Black House
derives its impenetrable
profile from its cladding
of black polypropylene
panels (left), while the
rear facade is charac-
terized by a high level of
transparency (right).

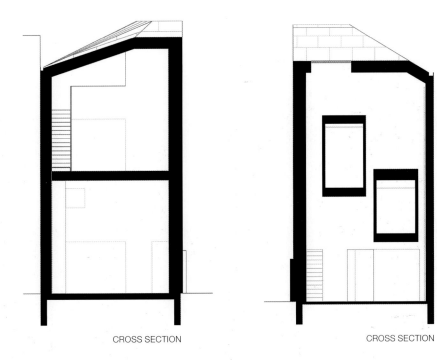

CROSS SECTION   CROSS SECTION

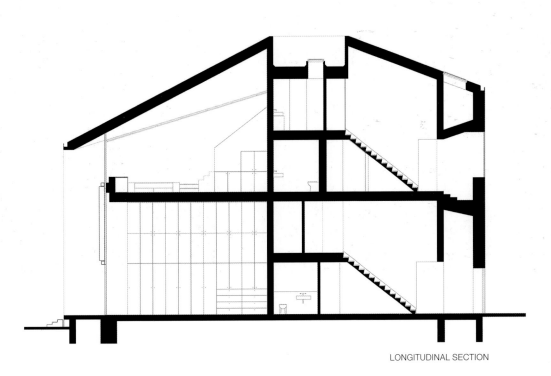

LONGITUDINAL SECTION

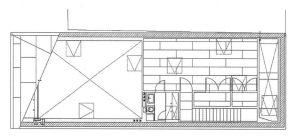

FIFTH FLOOR PLAN

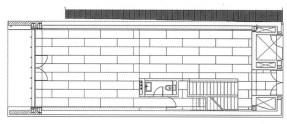

FOURTH FLOOR PLAN

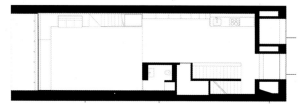

THIRD FLOOR PLAN

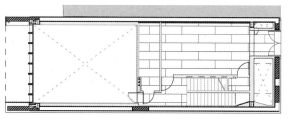

SECOND FLOOR PLAN

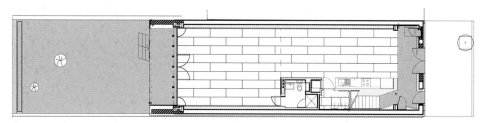

FIRST FLOOR PLAN

Among the meticulously crafted details found throughout the house are staircases with exquisitely formed concrete handrails illuminated with hidden fluorescent light (top left and right), custom millwork on the staircase in the living room (bottom left), and custom-formed concrete counters and sink in the kitchen (bottom right).

55

Left: Two artists'
studios each occupy
their own floor, one on
the attic level and,
here, at ground level.
Opposite: Both of
the double-height
studios feature sepa-
rate offices.

FERGUSON & SHAMAMIAN ARCHITECTS
BERESFORD APARTMENT
NEW YORK, NEW YORK

Architects Mark Ferguson and Oscar Shamamian have established themselves as masters of classical and traditional idioms, with projects ranging in style from neo-Palladian to Spanish Colonial revival. And the commission to redesign this palatial apartment in Manhattan's famed Beresford building, a landmark on Central Park West, would seem to demand a particularly robust demonstration of the stylistic flourishes and virtuoso craftsmanship for which the architects are so well known. However, the clients wished the apartment to be a suitable showcase for their substantial collection of contemporary art while still keeping in the spirit of the architectural pedigree of the 1929 Beresford, designed by Emery Roth in his inimitable streamlined traditional style. Undeterred by the apparent paradox at the heart of the commission, the architects were faced with another unusual condition, though one that would be irresistible for any New York architect: the apartment occupied five levels—floors twenty-one through twenty-five—in one of the building's three iconic towers.

The architects developed a clear, elegantly simple design strategy to address the unique complexities presented by the project. First, they approached the apartment as if it were a five-story townhouse, respecting its composition as a series of discrete rooms rather than as an opportunity to create loftlike spaces by tearing down walls. This meant that in many ways the organization of the rooms would remain unchanged, with living room, dining room, kitchen, and library on the first floor, and bedrooms and terraces on the second and third floors, while a light-filled family room was introduced on the fourth floor (an attic occupies the uppermost floor). But though their overall organization was unaltered, the circulation between the interior spaces was reconfigured to create a sense of openness and fluidity fully in keeping with contemporary tastes. For the public spaces on the first level, the architects repositioned doorways so that they align with each other, establishing a series of interior views. The doorways also were widened and their height extended nearly to the ceiling; their new arrangement and dimensions unify the rooms visually and allow them to share light and views.

The architects also refined the details of the space, removing moldings to accommodate large canvases and simplifying the remaining crown moldings and baseboards. This campaign of subtle subtraction extends to the windows, door surrounds, and even the ceilings, where $1/8$- or $1/4$-inch variations at the perimeter add finely nuanced depth and dimension. Similarly refined craftsmanship was employed on the staircases linking all five floors, surely the most spectacular intervention undertaken by the architects for this project. They conceived a series of sculptural stairs that turn and curve within the relatively constrained space allotted to them, and the detailing of the stairs further emphasizes their sculptural quality: the side rails and undersides of the solid white staircases are brushed smooth, and flat bronze handrails serve as an exquisite finish.

For the redesign of this palatial apartment in Manhattan's famed Beresford building, architects Mark Ferguson and Oscar Shamamian retained the overall organization of the interior spaces while reconfiguring circulation to create a sense of openness and fluidity fully in keeping with contemporary tastes.

The remarkable
apartment occupies
five floors in one of
the building's iconic
towers, and the system
of staircases linking all
five floors comprises a
spectacular intervention
by the architects.

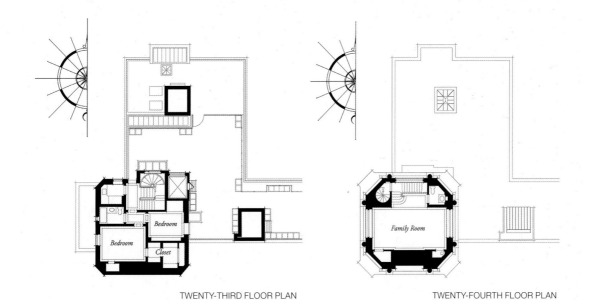

TWENTY-THIRD FLOOR PLAN

TWENTY-FOURTH FLOOR PLAN

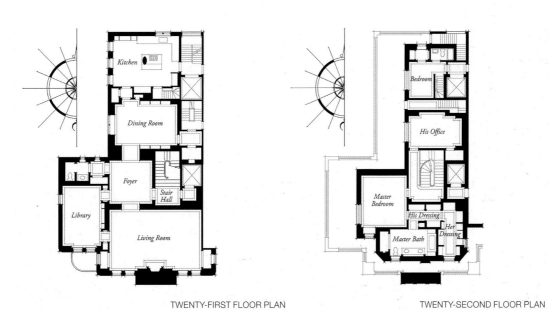

TWENTY-FIRST FLOOR PLAN

TWENTY-SECOND FLOOR PLAN

Within the relatively constrained spaces allotted to them, the staircases turn and curve in sculptural fashion, revealing such details as smooth-brushed side rails accented with flat bronze handrails.

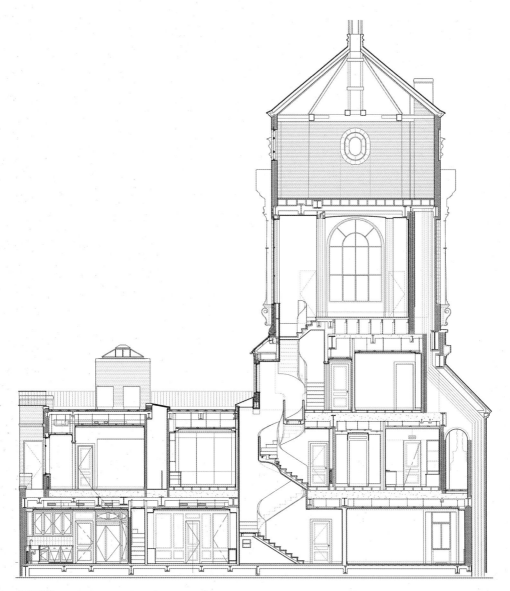

SECTION

One of the three
spectacular arched
windows of the
double-height family
room (following
pages) overlooks
the roof terrace.

The architects removed
or simplified mold-
ings and baseboards
in a campaign of
subtle subtraction
that extended to the
ceilings, where 1/8- or
1/4-inch variations at
the perimeter add finely
nuanced depth and
dimension, as in the
dining room (left) and
kitchen (opposite).

1100 ARCHITECT
BROOKLYN BROWNSTONE
BROOKLYN, NEW YORK

This five-story, thirty-foot-wide brownstone in the storied neighborhood of Brooklyn Heights is one of three adjacent and identical Gothic Revival townhouses. Comprising some 7,200 square feet, the house offered its new owners copious space and stately proportions but also a cluttered array of rooms, including a separate rental unit occupying the house's basement level. Juergen Riehm of the award-winning firm 1100 Architect, based in New York and Frankfurt, set out to integrate the house's interior spaces in a manner consistent with the lifestyle of a young family in the twenty-first century and to open those spaces up to the house's rear garden.

Among the first of the architect's priorities was the reconceptualization of a two-story structure projecting into the garden area from the house's rear facade. With few windows and closed off from the adjacent garden, the projection was transformed into an aluminum-and-glass pavilion housing the husband's study on the basement level and the kitchen on the main level. An exterior staircase from the garden up to the main level further integrates the house's public spaces with the garden. That spirit of openness informed the architect's approach to the house's interior spaces, where the introduction of natural light and flowing spaces was the guiding principle.

The house's main floor, up the front stoop from street level, contains the house's public spaces: living room, dining room, and kitchen. The adjacent living room and dining room form a continuous sequence, thanks to the expansive archway between the two rooms, which together span from the front to the rear of the house. The kitchen occupies the second level of the two-story aluminum-and-glass pavilion extending into the rear garden, a model of lightness, transparency, and twenty-first-century domesticity. Additionally, both the kitchen and dining room access a small terrace with stairs down to the garden at the rear of the house. The garden is accessed directly through his-and-her studies on the basement level—his occupying the bottom level of the rear pavilion, and hers at the rear of the main structure of the house. The basement level also accommodates a spacious guest room. Above the basement and main levels, the private domain of the house emerges. On the second floor are an intimate media room and a generously proportioned master suite—with two capacious walk-in closets, the ultimate New York luxury—which accesses a rustic, ecologically sustainable garden on the rooftop of the rear pavilion. The third floor is given over to the children's bedrooms, and finally the attic level was opened up to create a loftlike recreation room illuminated by a newly enlarged skylight.

As part of the renovation of one of three identical Gothic Revival townhouses, 1100 Architect reconfigured a dark, cluttered exterior two-story structure to become a light-filled glass and aluminum pavilion.

71

The rear pavilion is
only part of a renovation
that addressed all of
the townhouse's five
levels; an exterior
staircase from the
garden up to the main
level helps integrate the
house's public spaces
with the garden.

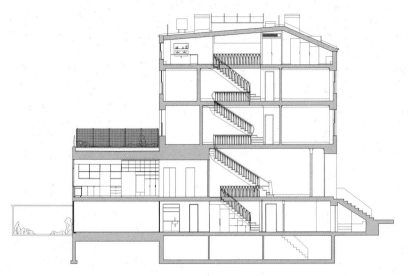

SECTION

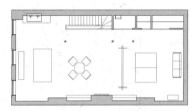

FOURTH FLOOR PLAN

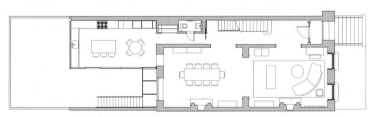

FIRST FLOOR PLAN

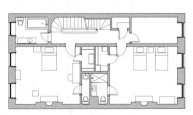

THIRD FLOOR PLAN

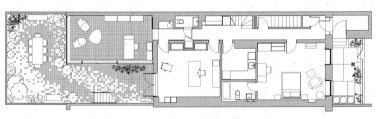

BASEMENT LEVEL

SECOND FLOOR PLAN

A spirit of openness informed the architect's approach to the house's interior spaces, where the introduction of natural light and flowing spaces was the guiding principle.

Opposite: The adjacent living room and dining room form a continuous sequence from the front to the rear of the house. Left: The architects integrated period details such as decorative moldings with a contemporary sense of openness.

Left: In the second-floor master suite the architects introduced a wall of floor-to-ceiling windows as well as spacious walk-in closets.
Opposite: The fourth-floor attic level was opened up to create a loftlike recreation room illuminated by a newly enlarged skylight.

Opposite: The newly constructed staircase between the basement and first levels features built-in storage space.
Left: The basement level accommodates his-and-her studies, his occupying the bottom level of the rear pavilion (top) and hers at the rear of the main structure of the house (bottom).

Opposite: At the main
level, the garden-facing
pavilion contains the
kitchen, which is a
model of lightness and
transparency.
Left: Above the kitchen
is a landscaped roof
terrace.

83

ANNABELLE SELLDORF
EAST VILLAGE TOWNHOUSE
NEW YORK, NEW YORK

Since establishing her practice in 1988, architect Annabelle Selldorf has achieved considerable expertise in designing spaces for world-class cultural institutions that are notable not only for their elegance but also for the intelligence and precision of their planning, among them the Neue Galerie Museum for German and Austrian Art and multiple art galleries in New York and London including Gagosian Gallery and Haunch of Venison. So it is not surprising that this townhouse, commissioned by a couple who are art collectors, should exhibit the same high degree of clarity and finish as those illustrious venues. What is unexpected is the warmth of the spaces contained within the house's four main floors. Stepping into this townhouse, one enters a meticulously planned series of spaces conceived for maximum usefulness, but it is a world far removed from the world of austere museum and gallery spaces.

The house is also set far away from the rarefied quarters of the city's elite that make up the Upper East Side. Rather, the clients presented Selldorf with an apartment house in Manhattan's East Village, a onetime center of the gritty creative scene of the 1970s and 1980s that, however gentrified it has become, still has its rough and ready veneer. To this erstwhile warren of spaces, Selldorf conceived of a design that would maintain a strong sense of the texture and details of a nineteenth-century structure while introducing open, light-filled spaces for a program that includes five bedrooms, a fluid public zone for entertaining, and generous, discrete private zones for the clients' family to gather. Joining these spaces is an understated, attenuated staircase that winds the entire height of the house beneath a massive skylight, providing not only elegant means of circulation through the house but also precious natural illumination.

The ground-floor entrance is a deceptively simple prelude to the breathtaking spaces to come, beginning with the expansive kitchen, occupying the rear of the ground floor and opening to the garden through two sets of oversized, arched French doors, flooding the space with life. Organized around a large fireplace, the kitchen is the house's literal as well as metaphorical hearth, and the stone tile floors add to the room's remarkable sense of warmth. The sculptural stair leads up to the house's main public zone, which is comprised of the expansive living and dining rooms, as well as a library. The dining room is positioned as a sort of overscaled stair landing, and its openness to the living room and to the light-giving stairwell ensure that the entire floor retains none of the darkness and closeness associated with New York living spaces. The third floor offers another space at its stair landing, this time a common space for the clients' children to gather around all things digital and around which their bedrooms are organized. The house's entire top floor is dedicated to the master bedroom suite, which is distinguished by exposed rough-hewn beams that extend into the spacious and luxurious bathroom, which is finished in marble walls and, in addition to a claw-footed tub and outsize glass shower, offers a sauna and wooden cold plunge tub.

Architect Annabelle Selldorf's transformation of an apartment house maintains a strong sense of the texture and details of a nineteenth-century structure while introducing open, light-filled spaces, including the large-scale living room (opposite), conceived for entertaining.

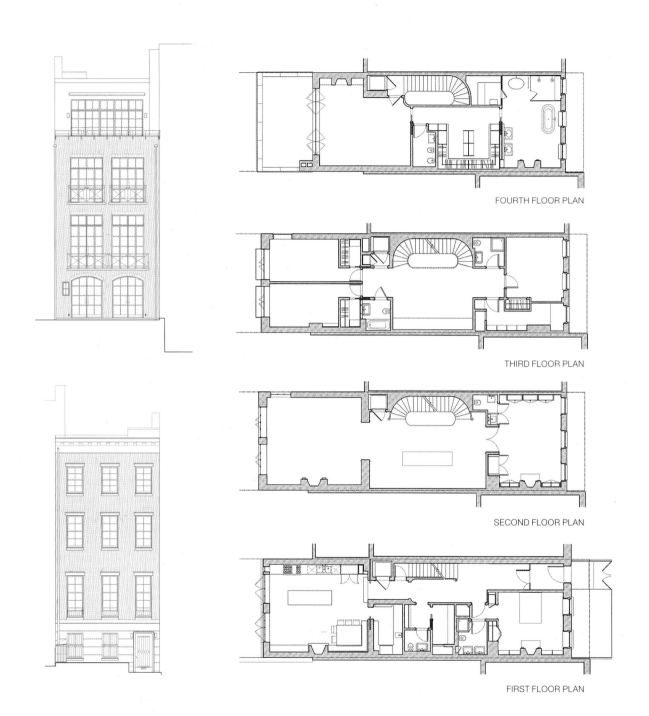

FOURTH FLOOR PLAN

THIRD FLOOR PLAN

SECOND FLOOR PLAN

FIRST FLOOR PLAN

The ground-floor entrance hall (top) leads to the expansive kitchen (bottom), which occupies the rear of the ground floor and opens to the garden through two sets of oversized, arched French doors; stone tile floors add to the room's remarkable sense of warmth.

The dining room is positioned as a sort of overscaled landing opposite the under-stated, attenuated staircase that winds the entire height of the house.

Both the public-
oriented, garden-facing
living room (left)
and the more private
family-oriented library
(opposite) feature
English marble mantels.

The house's entire top floor is dedicated to the master bedroom suite, which is distinguished by exposed rough-hewn beams, and which opens directly to a spacious stone-tiled terrace (opposite).

The master bedroom's wood beams extend into the master bathroom, which features a sauna, a wooden cold tub, and marble walls.

LOT-EK
WEINER TOWNHOUSE
NEW YORK, NEW YORK

For the renovation of a house for conceptual artist Lawrence Weiner and his wife, Alice, architects Ada Tolla and Giuseppe Lignano of the firm LOT-EK introduced their signature industrial chic aesthetic to the leafy environs of New York's West Village. Known for integrating recycled shipping containers, steel scaffolding, electrical conduits, and other repurposed industrial materials into their designs, whether residential or commercial, Tolla and Lignano sought to transform the three-story storefront building that Weiner purchased in 1990 as a live-work studio into a state-of-the-art townhouse not only with a studio but also space for Weiner's substantial archive. But unlike other such renovations in this and other highly desirable Manhattan neighborhoods, the Weiner house would not only reflect its architects' unique aesthetic but also fulfill the Weiners' desire to employ significant environmentally sustainable strategies in the reconstruction of their new home.

The architects virtually demolished the original structure, dating from 1910, retaining only its steel frame. The new construction stacks three open floors comprising a total of three thousand square feet, and adds a penthouse level composed of a vibrant green roof and a sunroom supporting photovoltaic panels. The architects allocated the living and working functions on alternating floors, so that the ground floor contains the kitchen and living room, the second floor the archive and office space, the third floor the master bedroom suite, and the cellar the artist's studio.

Each floor's sweeping open space is made possible by the positioning of the staircase across the house's rear facade, which is a dramatic translucent curtain wall employing highly insulating panels. Conversely, since local building regulations required that the house's front facade conform to a certain degree to the surrounding brick building fronts, the architects conceived of a conventional brick facade punctuated at each level by repurposed stainless steel truck bodies, each fulfilling a different function: kitchen bench on the ground floor, conference nook on the second floor, and bed platform on the third floor. In addition to the energy-efficient rear facade and solar-paneled penthouse, the architects employed a highly efficient pre-manufactured radiant floor heating system under rubber as well as wood floors, fluorescent and LED lighting, VOC-free paint, formaldehyde-free insulation, and energy-efficient appliances and mechanical/electrical equipment to realize a house that is as sustainable-minded as it is formally ambitious.

Architects Ada Tolla and Giuseppe Lignano of the firm LOT-EK brought their experience integrating recycled shipping containers, steel scaffolding, electrical conduits, and other repurposed industrial materials into their design for the renovation of a house for conceptual artist Lawrence Weiner and his wife, Alice.

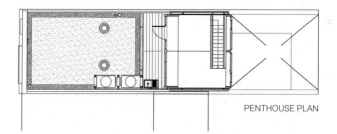

PENTHOUSE PLAN

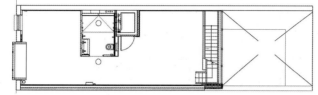

THIRD FLOOR PLAN

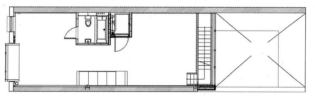

SECOND FLOOR PLAN

Weiner purchased the
house, in New York's
West Village, in 1990,
as a live-work studio,
and LOT-EK's brief was
to transform it into a
state-of-the-art town-
house with living space
and a studio as well
as space for Weiner's
substantial archive.

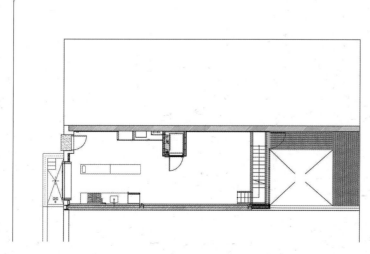

FIRST FLOOR PLAN

The ground floor of the house accommodates the entrance and kitchen at the front (right) and a living room/office at the rear (opposite), where the architects' industrial aesthetic is immediately apparent.

Opposite: The rooftop-level sunroom is punctuated by the vibrantly painted floor and ceiling.

Left: The house's staircase is positioned across the rear facade, which is a dramatic translucent curtain wall employing highly insulating panels.

Left: The ground-floor rear garden is overlooked by a catwalk extending from the second-level dining room.
Opposite: The architects added a penthouse level composed of a vibrant green roof and a sunroom supporting photovoltaic panels.

RICHARD MEIER
FIFTH AVENUE APARTMENT
NEW YORK, NEW YORK

This 2,500-square-foot apartment with priceless views of Central Park happens to occupy a full floor in one of the city's most legendary addresses, the Sherry-Netherland. What this dream apartment lacked, however, were the copious sunlight and fluid space desired by the clients, who turned to modernist master Richard Meier, working in collaboration with interior designer Rose Tarlow, to introduce a bit of downtown openness and informality to the 1927 landmark. The defining move in the service of this objective was for Meier to remove the walls separating the three contiguous rooms overlooking Fifth Avenue to create a single open space accommodating a living room, an adjacent sitting area for viewing movies and television (on a screen that artfully retracts behind a wall panel when not in use), and the dining room. Next to the dining room is a kitchen whose compactness is mediated by its total openness.

With the opening up of these front rooms, the apartment was effectively divided into two zones: open/public and closed/private, straddling the floor's central elevator core. Upon entering the apartment from a private elevator lobby, one is immediately in the midst of the centermost of the three spaces making up the open/public zone, the sitting/screening space. A short corridor immediately to the right leads to an office and a guest suite on the floor's north side. The south-facing private wing is entirely dedicated to a master bedroom suite with two full baths. It is accessed directly from the kitchen, a refreshingly unpretentious and practical arrangement of space in this grand venue. Equally practical is the master suite's placement on the south- rather than north-facing side of the floor, in order to maximize natural light.

Entrance from the elevator lobby is modulated by a set of louvered Anegre wood and glass door panels, and the pale yet warm-colored wood is employed throughout the apartment as part of a soft, unifying monochromatic palette. A low wooden bookcase lines the perimeter of the grand public space, and wood accents punctuate corridors and line the kitchen counter facing the dining room. Perhaps most spectacularly, the office and the foyer immediately entered from the elevators are completely paneled in honey-colored wood.

Modernist master Richard Meier recast a series of small rooms comprising a full floor in the landmark Sherry-Netherland, built in 1927, into a flowing 2,500-square-foot contemporary living space.

Meier removed the walls separating three contiguous rooms overlooking Fifth Avenue to create a single open space accommodating a living room, an adjacent sitting area for viewing movies and television, and a dining room.

The sitting area, viewed here with the dining area in the background, features a television screen that artfully retracts behind a wall panel when not in use.

PLAN

The kitchen is a model of efficiency, the compactness of which is mediated by its openness to the dining area.

In the guest bedroom (left) and guest bathroom (opposite) every inch of space has been accounted for by built-in storage or countertops.

Discreet yet elegant circulation space is fundamental to the effectiveness of the apartment's reconfigured spaces, as in the corridor adjacent to the guest bedroom and office (left) and the corridor intersecting the apartment's entrance (right).

Opposite: The elevator lobby features louvered Anegre wood and glass door panels. Left: Like the elevator lobby, the office is completely paneled in honey-colored wood.

JOHN PAWSON
OLD TOWN APARTMENT
GHENT, BELGIUM

John Pawson's name has virtually become a byword for highly refined minimalist design since he established his practice in 1981. He has applied his reductively sophisticated aesthetic to a range of types, from iconic retail spaces for Calvin Klein in the 1990s to a series of ecclesiastical commissions beginning with the seminal Nový Dvůr Monastery in the Czech Republic in 2004. Among this variety of projects has been a series of residential commissions that in many cases represent the prefect distillation of the principle of simplicity that characterizes Pawson's work regardless of scale. Such is the case with this large duplex apartment in the historical center of Ghent.

The apartment occupies the ground and second floor of a building on the Korenlei, the promenade along the River Lys in the oldest part of the city, and Pawson's brief was to create spaces for both living and working in a configuration that would allow each to function completely independently as well as together. Additionally preservation requirements determined that this introduction of contemporary spaces would need to be executed within the existing shell of the historic building, allowing no alterations to its exterior facade. To that end Pawson has created a series of generously scaled, well-proportioned spaces whose geometries are determined by the building's existing spaces and fenestration but whose circulation suggests flowing connectedness while retaining discrete rooms.

One enters the apartment at its upper floor, where greater ceiling height and larger windows led Pawson to reserve this level for the main living spaces and master bedroom. Here a library doubles as the apartment's entry foyer, and opens on either side to the master bedroom and the living room. The thresholds between these three rooms have been aligned with each other and positioned on an axis with a central window in the living room to create a series of interior views that visually unify the spaces. Adjacent to the main living space is a corridor leading to the kitchen—cordoned off from the living spaces in traditional fashion but articulated with sleek, state-of-the-art finishes—and to a monastic staircase that winds down to the lower level. Here the spaces are dominated by a large work studio, around which are arranged a small kitchen and a spacious guest suite, and the floors are rendered in polished concrete, a material fully expressive of Pawson's ethos of simplicity, utility, and elegance.

This apartment designed by John Pawson occupies two floors in a building in Ghent's historic center, with the lower level distinguished by polished concrete flooring, a material expressive of Pawson's design ethos of simplicity.

Adjacent to the long table that dominates the lower-level studio space is a full kitchen, which along with the floor's guest suite comprises a separate residence if needed.

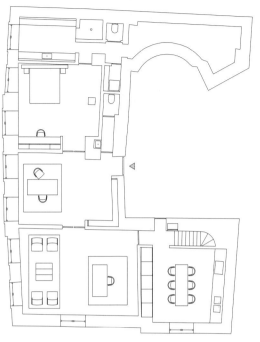

UPPER LEVEL PLAN

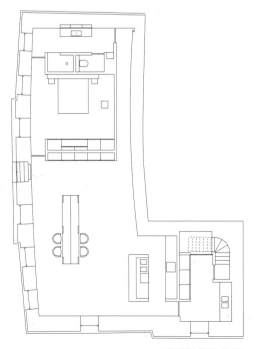

LOWER LEVEL PLAN

The apartment occupies the ground and second floor of a building on the Korenlei, the promenade along the River Lys in the oldest part of the city.

Left: The primary living spaces, such as the living room, here, are located on the apartment's upper level to take advantage of its high ceilings and large windows.
Right: The kitchen is cordoned off and proportioned like a traditional kitchen, with room for a full dining table, but has sleek, state-of-the-art finishes.

127

The master bathroom is outfitted with gray lava stone counters, which contribute to the restrained yet rich material palette used throughout the residence.

Left: Throughout
the apartment, built-in
funishings and light-
ing maximize spatial
efficiency and visual
effectiveness, as
in the master bedroom.
Right: The library
serves as the visitor's
first point of entry into
the apartment.

The Brick Weave House derives its name from the intricate two-story brick screen wall at its street front, behind which lies a garden and the entrance to the 3,250-square-foot house.

STUDIO GANG ARCHITECTS
BRICK WEAVE HOUSE
CHICAGO, ILLINOIS

Named for the intricate two-story brick screen wall at its street front, the Brick Weave House offers more than just a structurally ambitious facade. Studio Gang Architects, headed by Jeanne Gang, have created a spatially complex and formally witty structure in Chicago's West Town. The eponymous brick-weave wall was derived from the existing house on the site, from which the roof and front walls were removed, due to earlier fire damage, leaving space for a front garden bounded by the double-height filigreed brick wall, a challenging engineering feat that casts hexagonal light patterns onto the interior floors during the day and creates the effect of a delicate lantern at night. However, at the heart of the 3,250-square-foot house is the climate-controlled, showcase-like, skylit garage that accommodates the clients' collectible cars and motorcycles and directly accesses the house's spacious dining room cum entrance hall.

What follows is an unexpected progression through a corridor that doubles as a narrow galley kitchen to a small library and, two steps up, an expansive double-height living room. The result is a series of discrete spaces that fluidly engage one another to create the venue for entertaining desired by the clients. To further facilitate the ground-floor spaces' public function, the architect installed low-cost aluminum-and-frosted-glass Ikea wardrobes along the house's west wall, extending through the dining room/entrance all the way through the kitchen/corridor. In addition to providing copious, compactly organized storage overall, this strategy allows for the absence of overhead cabinets in the kitchen and the concealment of the refrigerator and other appliances, giving the space a sleek gallery-like quality. Additional storage space as well as generous laundry and mechanical space are tucked away in a service core around which the main public rooms are arrayed.

In the soaring living room, another dramatic sequence of progression emerges, this one characterized by expansion rather than the sequence of compression through the low-ceilinged kitchen/corridor. A flight of dark wood stairs ascends to an open mezzanine-level family room. Just beyond this first stairway, down a short corridor past a guest bedroom/study, is visible another flight of stairs, creating a dramatic sequence of ascension. At the pinnacle of this sequence is the master bedroom suite, which overlooks the front garden through a wall of floor-to-ceiling windows. Like the dining room immediately below as well as the grand-scale living room, the master suite extends across the entire width of the house and enjoys limitless natural light, as well as the privacy afforded by the architect's virtuoso brick screen.

The double-height filigreed brick wall casts hexagonal light patterns onto the interior floors during the day and creates the effect of a delicate lantern at night.

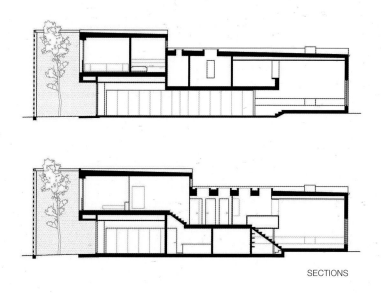

SECTIONS

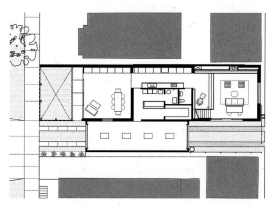

FIRST FLOOR PLAN

SECOND FLOOR PLAN

One enters the house directly into the dining room, which also directly accesses the showcase-like, skylit garage that accommodates the clients' collectible cars and motorcycles.

From the dining room cum entrance hall an unexpected progression leads through a corridor that doubles as a narrow galley kitchen (right) to the soaring double-height living room, where an impressive staircase leads to the bedroom level (opposite).

Left: The kitchen/ entrance corridor opens onto a small library, which in turn leads two steps up to the expansive living room. Opposite: The master bedroom overlooks the walled garden at the front of the house.

SIMON JACOBSEN
JACOBSEN TOWNHOUSE
WASHINGTON, D.C.

Having collaborated on countless residential projects as a partner in Jacobsen Architecture, founded by his father, Hugh Newell Jacobsen, Simon Jacobsen was more than prepared to bring his great experience and expertise to the design of his own house, which entailed the radical recasting of a pair of townhouses dating from 1863. Situated in the historic neighborhood of Georgetown, in Washington, D.C., each of the two townhouses hosted a long series of occupants, though based on structural evidence unearthed during the reconstruction process Jacobsen suspects the houses were originally constructed as a single residence. In addition to the labored recombination of two historical structures, Jacobsen also had to contend with the presence of a 1,500-square-foot addition undertaken in the 1980s at the rear of one of the houses.

The single newly conceived house now comprises a total of four thousand square feet distributed among three levels. Jacobsen thoroughly upended the distribution of the interior spaces, particularly on the main floor, where he introduced an open flow of space while retaining a spirit of old-world decorum as well as the original staircases in each of the two original townhouses. Central to Jacobsen's bold reconception of the arrangement of the interior spaces was the introduction of a formal entry sequence, with much of the front facade given over to a long, wide corridor leading to a reception room, called the "treaty room" by Jacobsen in good-humored reference to its largely ceremonial function. But aside from creating a space for formal entertaining, the introduction of this treaty room and its entry corridor also created a buffer between the street front and the other rooms on the main floor, the living room and library. The living room has been sequestered to the very rear of the house, in the 1980s-era addition, though it is separated from the 1860s-era structure by a mere two steps up, spanning the width of the room; the living room is also masterfully integrated with the older structure thanks to its access to the original 1860s-era staircase. The library accesses the other of the two original staircases as well as a rear terrace with a spiral staircase leading down to the house's garden, one level below.

At the garden level, the house's interior spaces comprise a formal dining room, an office, a home theater (the perfect function for the one space in the house cut off from natural light), and the kitchen. Like the entry corridor placed directly above, the kitchen spans the front facade in the manner of a long gallery, an unusual arrangement for a kitchen space but which here seems resourceful and urbane. The uppermost of the house's three levels is devoted to three bedrooms and an ample dressing room. The master bedroom is the most private of the three, occupying the 1980s addition at the rear of the house. The entire addition's facade was removed at all three levels and replaced to accommodate elegant, relatively narrow floor-to-ceiling casement windows that were custom designed by Jacobsen, as were the library's square white egg-crate bookshelves, a longstanding signature of Jacobsen Architecture.

Architect Simon Jacobsen introduced an open flow of space while retaining a spirit of old-world decorum to the renovation of a pair of townhouses in Georgetown dating from 1863 to become his own residence.

In addition to combining two historical structures, the project required Jacobsen to integrate a 1,500-square-foot addition undertaken in the 1980s at the rear of one of the houses.

FRONT ELEVATION

REAR ELEVATION

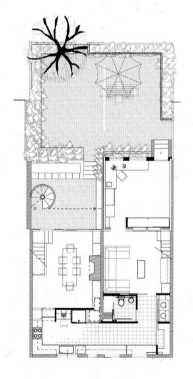

BASEMENT PLAN

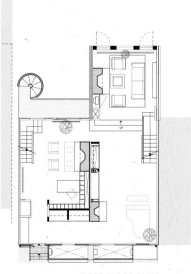

FIRST FLOOR PLAN

SECOND FLOOR PLAN

Right: In addition to completely reconfiguring the arrangement of spaces and the organization of circulation, Jacobsen also retained the original staircases in each of the two original townhouses. Opposite: A view from the library to the living room, which occupies the rear 1980s-era addition.

Opposite: The "treaty room," which Jacobsen designed not only to be a public-oriented space for entertaining but also to serve as a buffer between the street front and the other rooms on the main floor, the living room and library.
Left: In the library, the custom-designed, square white egg-crate bookshelves are a long-standing signature of Jacobsen Architecture.

The master bedroom
occupies the second
level of the 1980s-
era addition, immedi-
ately above the
living room, and over-
looks the rear garden.

ALLIED WORKS
ARCHITECTURE
NYC LOFT
NEW YORK, NEW YORK

Allied Works Architecture, headed by Brad Cloepfil, has its identity firmly rooted in its West Coast locale, thanks in large part to the iconic headquarters it designed for Wieden + Kennedy, in the architecture firm's hometown of Portland. But far from being a local wonder, Allied Works can claim a series of high-profile projects throughout the United States, including St. Louis's Contemporary Art Museum, the Clyfford Still Museum in Denver, the Seattle Art Museum, the University of Michigan Museum of Art, as well as the National Music Centre of Canada, in Calgary, under construction. And one of the most talked about of these projects, the Museum of Arts and Design, brought Cloepfil to New York, where in 2004 he established an East Coast outpost. With the NYC Loft, designed for a pair of art collectors, Cloepfil has proven himself to be thoroughly at home in the city.

The loft comprises 13,000 square feet on the top three floors of a historic building in the TriBeCa district of lower Manhattan. Such vast amounts of space gave the architects the latitude to create an extraordinarily intricate section composed of a series of voids in the form of double-height interior spaces and carved-out open courtyards. The result is a myriad of spaces of varying scale, and the architects developed a custom cast-aluminum finish for the walls employed together with warm white oak wood ceilings to create a unified interior.

The residence's lowest level, on the building's eighth floor, is devoted to guest accommodations, while one level up, the building's ninth floor, is dedicated to five bedrooms. Connecting this floor to the tenth floor is a sinuous, grandly scaled switchback stairway, while the ninth-floor stair landing overlooks a sitting room on the eighth-floor guest level. The tenth floor is given over to the residence's public spaces, including living and dining spaces conceived for large-scale entertaining, a marble-finished kitchen featuring a ceiling composed entirely of clear glass, and more intimate family-oriented zones. Punctuating these various spaces and levels are courtyard gardens designed by artist Paula Hayes; the architects also collaborated with artist Doug Aitken on the creation of kaleidoscopic mirrored light wells. The entire residence is crowned by the addition of a penthouse sunroom and garden at roof level.

This loft designed by Allied Works Architecture, headed by Brad Cloepfil, comprises 13,000 square feet on the top three floors of a historic building, affording sweeping views of the surrounding TriBeCa district of lower Manhattan and beyond.

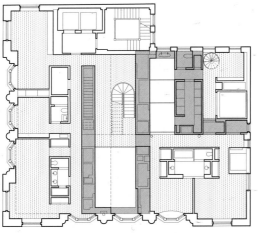

NINTH FLOOR PLAN

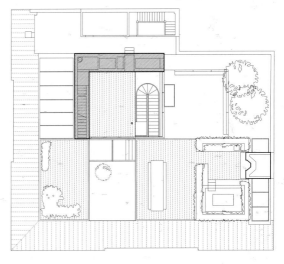

ELEVENTH FLOOR PLAN

The loft's vast amounts of space allowed the architects to create an intricate series of voids in the form of double-height interior spaces and carved-out open courtyards.

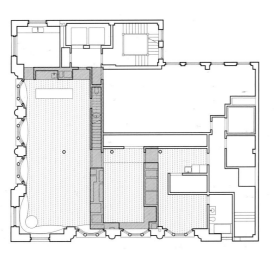

EIGHTH FLOOR PLAN

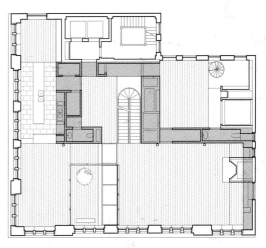

TENTH FLOOR PLAN

A generous open courtyard lies between the living room and, in the background, the dining room, which are linked by a glassed-in corridor.

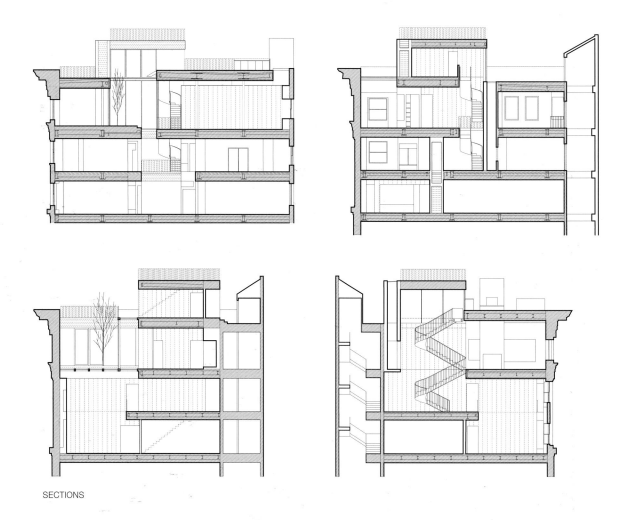

SECTIONS

In the living room, and throughout the loft, the architects developed a custom cast-aluminum finish for the walls, which is nicely contrasted by warm white oak wood ceilings.

Right: In addition to pockets of outdoor space, the architects were able to use the loft's expansive spaces and multiple levels to create soaring interior volumes, such as the double-height sitting room that doubles as a miniature basket-ball court.

Opposite: The kitchen is distinguished by an array of rich materials, including the aluminum and white oak used throughout the apart-ment as well as white marble counters, while the ceiling is composed entirely of glass panes that open to the roof terrace on the loft's uppermost level.

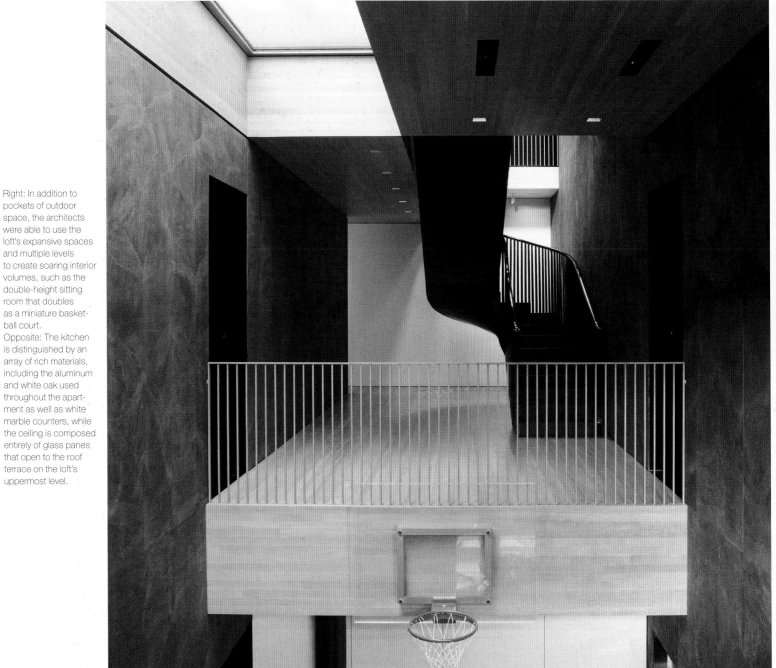

GUS WÜSTEMANN
CRUSCH ALBA LOFT
BARCELONA, SPAIN

Named Crusch Alba Loft, after the Swiss Romansh for "white cross," this flexible living space designed by architect Gus Wüstemann for himself and his family presents an innovative solution to the distribution of domestic functions by eschewing rooms in the traditional sense. The two-thousand-square-foot space occupies the second floor of a building dating from circa 1860 in Barcelona's Gothic Quarter, the old city center. Here centuries-old apartment houses front extremely narrow streets, making natural light a scarce amenity in the often-warrenlike spaces behind the district's Gothic and neoclassical facades.

In the renovation of a 2,000-square-foot apartment into a loft for himself and his family, architect Gus Wüstemann sought to maximize spatial fluidity and natural illumination as well as to retain a sense of the palimpsest of finishes that accrued in the structure over the decades.

Wüstemann addressed this deficit of natural light by devising a spatial organization that maximizes fluidity and openness. With a relatively conventional living room and dining room at the front of the apartment, where floor-to-ceiling-height windows open to shallow balconies, the apartment's sleeping spaces were relegated to the rear portion of the floor, where the only sources of light were three light wells. Therefore Wüstemann elected to eliminate traditional walls and corridors, to be replaced by a cross-shaped intervention that would provide circulation as well as space for all domestic service functions (e.g., kitchen and bathroom spaces). Here the eponymous white cross is delineated in a floor of white epoxy, underneath which is provided state-of-the-art radiant heating. Kitchen appliances and fixtures are concealed behind white cabinetry; lavatories are tucked into cubicles behind white sliding doors. A large white shower occupies the farthest end down the long, white corridor composing one arm of the cross.

Around this bold intervention are arranged a series of flexible spaces divisible by sliding panels and capable of transforming the open loft into a three-bedroom apartment, though these spaces are not strictly speaking bedrooms but, rather, multifunctional spaces. For instance, a wooden platform serves as a favorite play area while also concealing a large bathtub beneath removable panels. And the children's sleeping areas are wherever they lay their foldable mattresses.

The pristine, brightly illuminated white cross presents a spectacular contrast with the exposed stone and raw finishes of the surrounding living spaces. These include deliberately exposed beams, plaster, wallpaper fragments, and an old fresco behind the dining room table. To these layers of finishes accrued over years Wüstemann has added a new layer of wooden elements, specifically a wooden floor that extends up the walls to the height of traditional wainscoting and conceals ambient lighting that illuminates the architectural palimpsest characterizing this unique domicile.

Right: The loft is located in a building dating from c. 1860 in Barcelona's Gothic Quarter, the old city center, where natural light is a scarce amenity.

Opposite: The front of the apartment features the dwelling's most generous light source, a series of three floor-to-ceiling-height windows that open to shallow balconies, and this is where Wüstemann situated the main living and dining areas.

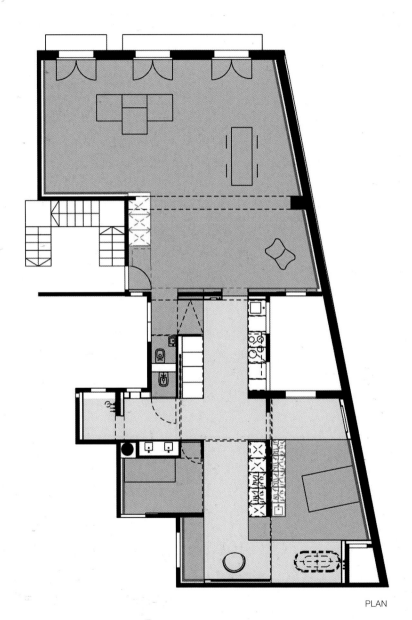

Wüstemann located
the sleeping spaces at
the apartment's rear,
with the white-clad
kitchen serving also as
a corridor between the
two zones.

PLAN

Crusch alba is Swiss Romansh for "white cross," a form that is delineated in a floor of white epoxy and appliances and fixtures concealed behind white cabinetry; lavatories are tucked into cubicles behind white sliding doors.

Opposite: Throughout the apartment Wüstemann introduced wooden elements, including a floor that extends up the walls to the height of traditional wainscoting and conceals ambient lighting.
Right: The large bathtub adjacent to the master bedroom can be concealed beneath removable panels to serve as a platformed play area.

Contrasting the brightly illuminated white cross are exposed stone and raw finishes that include deliberately exposed beams, plaster, and wallpaper fragments.

DEAN/WOLF ARCHITECTS
INVERTED WAREHOUSE/TOWNHOUSE
NEW YORK, NEW YORK

The neighborhood of TriBeCa in Manhattan is characterized by nineteenth-century industrial buildings that began to be converted into residences in the 1970s and '80s. While these are most typically loft spaces sprawling across a single floor, the commission received by Dean/Wolf Architects for this residence occupying the top five floors of a relatively narrow six-story warehouse building offered a unique opportunity to introduce the organizational principles of a multilevel townhouse to an industrial structure. However, the unmediated arrangement of spaces in the manner of a conventional townhouse would not have been practical. For instance, the building's siting within a close-fitting industrial urban fabric meant that the outdoor space present at the rear of the typical townhouse would not be available here, which led the architects on a path that inverted inside space and outside space and, ultimately, inverted the organization of space from top to bottom.

In order to recover the garden space that was not available at a garden level, the architects created a pair of interlocking voids that extended through the house's floors from a single large opening at the roof garden level. Additional outdoor space is provided by a large terrace carved out of a corner of the house's uppermost full floor. The first of the two interior large voids extends down two levels to an open-air courtyard. Adjacent to this courtyard, on the house's fourth floor, is a glass-enclosed void, which admits natural light from the fourth-floor courtyard down to another interior courtyard on the third floor. Additional, more modestly scaled interior voids, enclosed and double-height, further distribute natural light to the second and first levels. Around this series of interior voids—both indoor and outdoor, and all naturally illuminated from above—the architects have arrayed interior spaces at remarkably varying scales as well as a formally complex network of multiple staircases, which maintain a spectacular sculptural presence throughout the house.

The architects created another inversion with their decision to organize the building's floors so that the most open, airy spaces would be at the top, thereby maximizing access to the natural light that would be filtered down through the house. This logically dictated that the more open, public zones would be located on the uppermost floors, with privacy and a sense of enclosure increasing as one moves down floor by floor from the entry elevator lobby and main living room on the fifth floor. The fourth floor is given over to the expansive dining room and kitchen, and the third floor is dedicated to the master bedroom suite and an additional bedroom. These three floors are linked not only by the courtyards carved into their innermost zones but also by no less than three separate sculptural staircases. The remaining two floors contain additional bedrooms and a cavernous recreation space. Linking the multifarious spaces arrayed among five levels is a strong and consistent material palette composed of Cor-ten steel panels and brick for the walls, and polished concrete and, in some places, light-extending glass for the floors.

For this residence occupying the top five floors of a warehouse building, Dean/Wolf Architects inverted the organization of the typical townhouse and created garden space by way of a pair of interlocking voids that extend down through the house.

The architects located the most open, airy spaces at the top floors, with the fourth floor given over to the expansive dining room and kitchen.

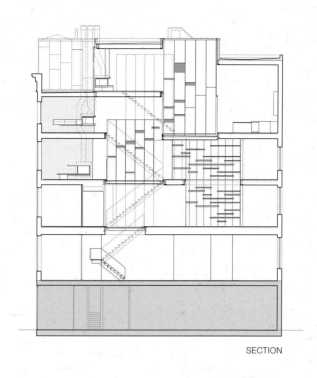

SECTION

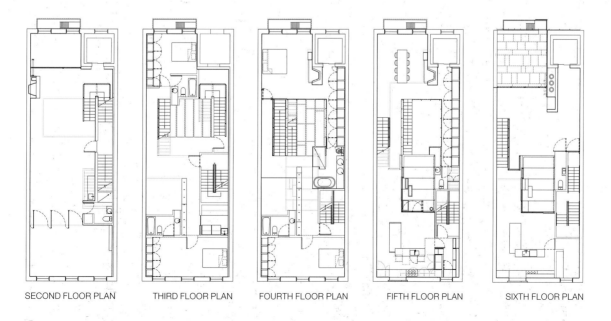

SECOND FLOOR PLAN   THIRD FLOOR PLAN   FOURTH FLOOR PLAN   FIFTH FLOOR PLAN   SIXTH FLOOR PLAN

Opposite: Cor-ten steel panels are employed throughout the loft, inside and out.
Right: In addition to being linked by the newly created courtyards carved into their innermost zones, the loft's various spaces are also linked by three separate sculptural staircases.

Unifying the loft's five
levels is a strong
and consistent material
palette that includes
Cor-ten steel panels
for the walls (left) and
light-extending glass
for the floors (opposite,
far left).

Left: The use of polished concrete floors and Cor-ten steel wall panels extends to the bathrooms.
Opposite: Additional outdoor space is provided by a large terrace adjacent to the living room, carved out of a corner of the house's uppermost full floor.

LORCAN O'HERLIHY ARCHITECTS
FLYNN MEWS HOUSE
DUBLIN, IRELAND

The creation of the Flynn Mews House in Dublin is the result of a number of remarkable factors, first among which was the presence on the site of a neoclassical facade dating from 1847. The wall belonged to a carriage house that originally occupied the site, and though the client was entitled to tear down the old structure and replace it with a new construction, the architecturally significant nineteenth-century wall had to be preserved under local landmark regulations. Additionally, the new construction was required to be modern in its design and to present a clear formal contrast with the original wall. This condition led to the second remarkable feature of the project, which was the client's decision to turn to modernist architect Lorcan O'Herlihy, who just happens to be Los Angeles's most celebrated Irish expatriate architect.

O'Herlihy leapt at the chance to build in his native Ireland for the first time. Since the historically significant wall faces the rear of the site, rather than facing the street, O'Herlihy conceived of two structures on opposite sides of an interior courtyard, one wall of which would be the nineteenth-century facade. The first of the two structures comprises a sort of entrance pavilion. Facing the street, it presents a monolithic facade with a deep, large void leading to the house's entrance. One immediately enters the courtyard, facing the second, main structure—and it is here that observant visitors will note that they have actually passed through the preserved nineteenth-century facade. To the left, visitors see a glass bridge traversing an excavation exposing a level below grade to connect the entrance structure to the main structure, while immediately ahead lies the facade of the main structure, composed of a wall of floor-to-ceiling glass.

Together the two structures comprise 2,900 square feet of interior space. One enters the main structure into the expansive kitchen and dining space, beyond which is the main living space. Tucked away into a niche is a staircase leading down to a bedroom below grade, while the master bedroom suite rises a half level from the main living space. From the kitchen the glass bridge leads to the secondary structure, which contains a media room on the ground level and two bedrooms on the upper level. A simple but bold material palette creates a strong profile of the house's interior as well as exterior. Charcoal-tinted board-formed concrete is dramatically contrasted with glass and white plaster outside, while inside wood wall panels and ceilings contrast with stained concrete floors and white marble finishes.

A glass bridge connects the house's main structure to a smaller entrance pavilion, part of which is composed of a neoclassical facade dating from 1847, seen here through the dining space's floor-to-ceiling windows.

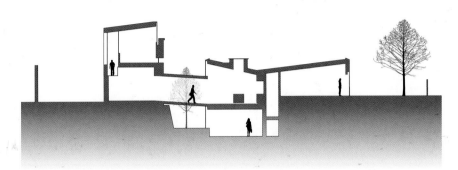

SECTION

The house's rear facade is characterized by an overall transparency with the living room and master bedroom open to the rear garden.

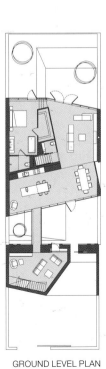

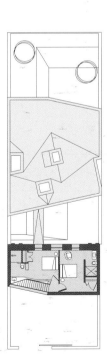

LOWER LEVEL PLAN

GROUND LEVEL PLAN

UPPER LEVEL PLAN

The smaller entrance
pavilion structure
presents a monolithic
facade with a deep,
large void leading to
the house's entrance.

Left: A view through the glass bridge from the kitchen to the secondary structure, which contains a media room on the ground level and two bedrooms on the upper level.
Opposite: The master bedroom occupies the house's main floor, facing the rear garden.

In the expansive kitchen and dining space, wood wall panels and ceilings contrast with stained concrete floors and white marble finishes.

Architect Rolf Bruggink in association with Zecc Architecten boldly painted the facade of his own three-story row house pitch black, lending the house its name, "Black Pearl," and affording it a powerful formal profile.

STUDIO ROLF.FR AND ZECC ARCHITECTEN
BLACK PEARL
ROTTERDAM, NETHERLANDS

When architect Rolf Bruggink took advantage of a program initiated by the city of Rotterdam to sell homes in economically depressed neighborhoods at below-market prices he found himself facing a derelict townhouse but also a great opportunity. In the three-story, 1,800-square-foot row house Bruggink had free rein to radically alter the interior as a showcase for his design sensibility, the audacity of which found its way to the building's facade as well. Completed in association with Zecc Architecten, the Black Pearl—as Bruggink dubbed the house, after the facade, which he made the bold move of painting pitch black—is an essay in formal risk and inventiveness, resulting in a modestly scaled home with a disproportionately powerful profile.

The house, which dated from the first decade of the twentieth century, was completely overrun with vegetation, and its interior wooden elements had rotted throughout. In light of the extreme distress of the existing interior, Bruggink decided to gut the entire structure, freeing him to conceive of a wholly original interior layout. Having given over the ground level to the workshop for his furniture design business, Bruggink situated all of the residential functions on the house's second and third floors as a series of open, even abstract spaces on varying levels and punctuated by unexpected openings between levels. The result is a spatially complex composition with a dizzying effect the architect likens to an engraving by M. C. Escher. The spaces' abstract quality is heightened by the absence of almost all bannisters and balcony railings.

Bruggink translated the ambitious and bold scope of the interior to the structure's unremarkable row house exterior as well. In addition to coating the brick facade in black oil paint, Bruggink covered over the existing windows and replaced them with clean-lined, metal-framed rectangular apertures of varying scales, one on the ground floor, one on the second floor, and one on the third. And even more boldly, he retained the formwork of the original windows so that the formal details of the original facade maintain a ghostly presence amid the radical interventions of the architect. Additionally, the house's one visible side facade is overlayed with a carpet of intensely green artificial turf. And the architect's crowning flourish of formal wit is represented by the newly constructed greenhouse structure on the roof, which houses not carefully cultivated vegetation but simply a luxurious bathtub.

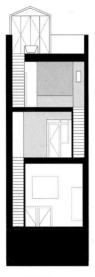

CROSS SECTION

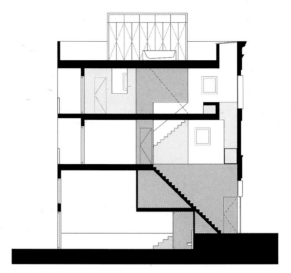

LONGITUDINAL SECTION

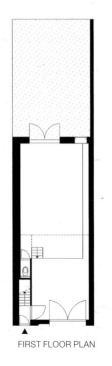

FIRST FLOOR PLAN

SECOND FLOOR PLAN

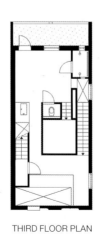

THIRD FLOOR PLAN

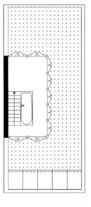

ROOF PLAN

One side of the
Black Pearl is
clad entirely in
artificial turf.

197

New windows have been punctured into the front facade, while the formwork of the original windows has been retained. The result is a ghostly presence on the exterior (left) and clean-lined apertures on the interior (right).

The house's interior comprises a spatially complex composition with a dizzying effect the architect likens to an engraving by M. C. Escher, and the spaces' abstract quality is heightened by the absence of almost all bannisters and balcony railings.

The house's living spaces are arranged on the second and third floors in a series of open, connected spaces, as with the living room and kitchen/dining room, pictured here.

Opposite: The structure's original brick walls have been retained in the living room, with one side painted white, along with the wood floors, and the other left exposed.

Left: A newly constructed timber box conceals wiring and piping and appears suspended between the living and dining rooms.

The entire ground
floor of the house is
reserved as a workshop
for Bruggink's furniture
design business and
opens onto the house's
rear garden.

BARBARA BESTOR
FLOATING BUNGALOW
VENICE, CALIFORNIA

Another dwelling in the dense Los Angeles enclave of Venice, the Floating Bungalow is a sunny and remarkably livable project designed by Barbara Bestor, a Los Angeles–based architect who has become strongly identified with the city in which she established her practice in 1995. Bestor is responsible for a host of designs for houses, commercial spaces, and studios for a largely creative clientele, and her book, *Bohemia Modern: Living in Silver Lake*, introduced a friendly Los Angeles brand of contemporary modernist living to the wider world. Her projects are characterized by the use of industrial or commercial materials, often at relatively low cost, and by a bold yet relaxed use of color. Her Floating Bungalow, a two-thousand-square-foot, two-level house commissioned by an advertising art director for a site on one of Venice's pedestrian-only thoroughfares, perfectly embodies the principles for which she has become so well known.

Taking her cue from the closely situated single-story bungalows that characterize the neighborhood, Bestor conceived of the house's upper level as a white bungalow-shaped "cloud" floating over a charcoal-colored ground level. The lower level's smaller footprint allows for the creation of a meticulously landscaped outdoor room adjacent to the front facade. Here the phrase "outdoor room" operates as much more than the standard euphemism for a patio or porch; rather, it reflects the openness that distinguishes the entire lower level, which is devoted to the house's public spaces—living room, dining room, kitchen, and even dedicated d.j. booth—all arranged as one continuously flowing space. Upstairs, the sleeping spaces are more discretely arranged, though here too Bestor has introduced transparency and fluidity. Beneath the relatively steeply pitched ceiling, the interior walls reach only eight feet high before being replaced by clear glass panels. Aside from this visual transparency, the master bedroom maximizes privacy, with a spacious en suite bath and a private balcony carved out of one of the house's front corners. The secondary bedroom, by contrast, has the long, narrow proportions of a dormitory and can easily be subdivided into two bedrooms.

The exterior of the lower level is clad in fiber panel siding and all the windows throughout the house were manufactured for commercial use. Inside, built-in bookshelves in the dining room and d.j. booth are composed of low-cost plywood, as is the custom-designed cabinetry in the kitchen, and the entire ground level is floored with concrete. The relative austerity of these materials is punctuated by bright yellow walls and vibrantly colored furniture. Color also provides a witty cultural reference in the matte-black-finished kitchen island, which mimics the technique of blacking out all detailing on customized cars (known as "murdering").

At the Floating Bungalow's front facade, the dining room opens to an adjacent garden that serves as an outdoor room.

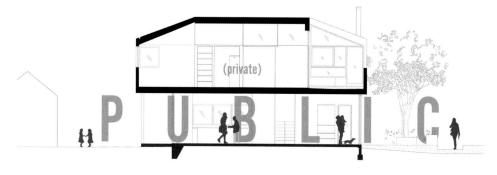

SECTION

Entry to the house, at far right, brings one directly into a large, free-flowing space accommodating living room, kitchen, and, pictured here, dining room, which features built-in bookshelves constructed of low-cost plywood.

SECOND FLOOR PLAN

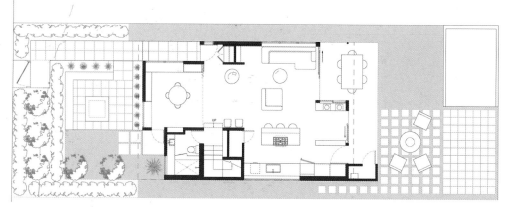

FIRST FLOOR PLAN

As in the dining room, the custom-designed cabinetry in the kitchen is built of plywood, while throughout the lower level flooring is composed of concrete.

Opposite: In the master bedroom, an understated, relatively low-cost material palette is punctuated by colorful furnishings.

Left: Beneath the relatively steeply pitched ceiling, the interior walls reach only eight feet high before being replaced by clear glass panels.

Right: A private balcony opening off the master bedroom and bathroom is carved out of one of the house's front corners.
Opposite: The house derives its name from the image of a pristine white structure appearing to float above a charcoal-colored ground level.

UNSTUDIO
ART COLLECTOR'S LOFT
NEW YORK, NEW YORK

The Amsterdam-based architecture firm UNStudio has proven itself as adept and comfortable applying its sinuous forms to commissions for private residences as for their higher-profile projects, including museums, theaters, and even an airport. Yet despite the demands of these large-scale projects, the firm, which is headed by Ben van Berkel and Caroline Bos, has continually engaged in the particular challenges presented by creating houses for a select group of fearless clients, most of them astute collectors of modern and contemporary art. These formally bold and structurally experimental essays, beginning with their seminal Mobius House of 1993, are relatively modest-scaled structures that manage to maintain the potency of the firm's most ambitious projects. With the commission to design this loft for an art collector, though, a new challenge emerged: having originally asked van Berkel to design a new house to be built in Connecticut, the client instead decided to renovate an expansive loft space in the heart of downtown Manhattan, presenting van Berkel with the task of translating UNStudio's sculptural vocabulary to the loft's fixed interior volume.

Van Berkel's first challenge was to negotiate the low, wide proportions of the loft's open interior space. He quickly turned this condition to his advantage, dividing the space into distinct zones, one of which would give over a disproportionate amount of the loft's nearly six thousand square feet to display the client's significant collection of modernist and contemporary art. Straddling either side of this gallery space are two long, narrow private zones—one containing the kitchen, storage space, and a guest bedroom, and one containing the master bedroom suite—while at either end of the open gallery space are two open living areas. The client's desire for a library similarly presented van Berkel with a challenge that he transformed into an opportunity, in this case a tour-de-force serpentine wall running to one side along the entire length of the loft's gallery space, creating a narrow, curving library and secondary exhibition space adjacent to the master bedroom suite.

The library's curving wall represents one element of the overall technical virtuosity brought by van Berkel and his team, suspended as it is from an existing beam in the loft's structure and touching the floor plane at only one point at its north end. Comparable technical skill has been applied to the creation of a luminous ceiling composed of 18,000 LED light sources mounted to the ceiling and concealed by a membrane of translucent white fabric. Tracks running through the fabric membrane allow for directed spotlighting; the complex network of LEDs can be programmed to provide a range of light quality from cool to warm tones; and the fabric membrane provides a sense of greater height within the space by creating an impression of limitlessness.

The built-in desk in the master bedroom reflects the sinuous forms that distinguish many of the projects designed by UNStudio, headed by Ben van Berkel and Caroline Bos.

A luminous ceiling composed of translucent white fabric conceals 18,000 LED light sources, with tracks running through the fabric membrane allowing directed spotlighting.

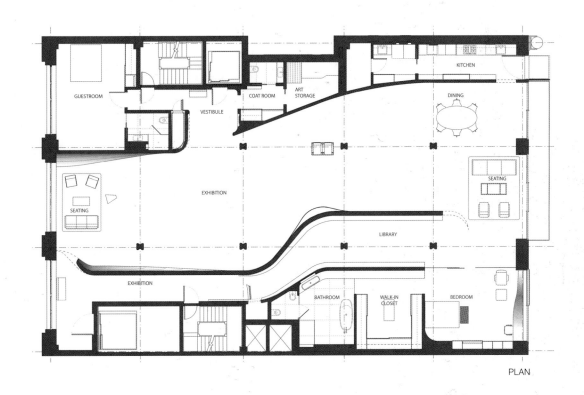

GUESTROOM

VESTIBULE

COAT ROOM

ART STORAGE

KITCHEN

DINING

SEATING

EXHIBITION

SEATING

LIBRARY

EXHIBITION

BATHROOM

WALK-IN CLOSET

BEDROOM

PLAN

Opposite: A dispro-
portionate amount of
the loft's nearly 6,000
square feet is given
over to display the
client's significant
collection of modernist
and contemporary art.
Left: Adjacent to the
large central gallery
space is tucked a
library and more inti-
mately scaled gallery.

223

The curving wall in the library and smaller gallery is suspended from an existing beam in the loft's structure, touching the floor plane at only one point at its north end.

The large central gallery space is straddled by two long, narrow private zones: one containing the kitchen and a guest bedroom (top right and opposite) and one containing the master bedroom and master bathroom (bottom right).

CHENCHOW LITTLE
SKYLIGHT HOUSE
SYDNEY, AUSTRALIA

The commission undertaken by architects Tony Chenchow and Stephanie Little to renovate this traditional terrace house not only required the introduction of three bedrooms, two bathrooms, and a new kitchen but also the meticulous preservation of the original house's facade. The house is situated in the Balmain neighborhood of Sydney, a leafy, densely populated, historically working-class enclave characterized by landmark-protected Victorian architecture. Behind the carefully restored gingerbread facade, the architects intervened with an inventive, wholly new construction composed of intricate layers of spaces on multiple levels organized around a central courtyard and illuminated by a complex system of skylights.

The architects first inverted the spatial arrangement of the original house by placing two bedrooms on the ground floor and an expansive, open living space on the second floor opening onto a balcony running the full width of the house's front facade. An intermediate floor at the level of the landing between the first and second floors was created toward the rear of the sloping site; it contains an open kitchen and dining space with access to a rear courtyard garden, and a staircase leading up to a master bedroom suite sequestered on its own floor. This arrangement effectively divides the house into two volumes connected by a smaller volume dedicated to the stairs between the first and intermediate levels and those linking the intermediate and second levels. These volumes are arranged around a central courtyard, which allows both the living space and the kitchen-dining space access to natural light at either end. Thanks to a sculptural exterior staircase, the courtyard is accessible from the second-level living space as well as from the kitchen-dining space, with which it shares the intermediate level.

Even more impressive than the carefully modulated variation in floor levels is the highly sculptural ceiling, which is composed of an intricate series of curves, folds, and gaps, these last giving the house its name. From the interior of the living space the skylights appear as a series of overscaled slats, though structurally they are composed of two large telescoping roof elements carved out of the roofline of the original house structure. Meanwhile, the ceiling of the kitchen-dining space, though closed, is just as expressive as that of the living space thanks to its long central arch and deep curves at either end. Contributing further to the house's formal power is the restrained, almost minimalist approach to materials, dominated by exposed cast concrete structural elements and flooring, sculpted white plaster on the ceiling, and contrasting rich gum wood cabinetry and wainscoting.

Behind a landmark-protected facade, architects Tony Chenchow and Stephanie Little introduced an intricate series of spaces on multiple levels organized around a central courtyard and illuminated by a complex system of skylights.

While from the street the Victorian row house appears virtually untouched, two large telescoping skylight structures have been carved out of the roofline of the original house structure.

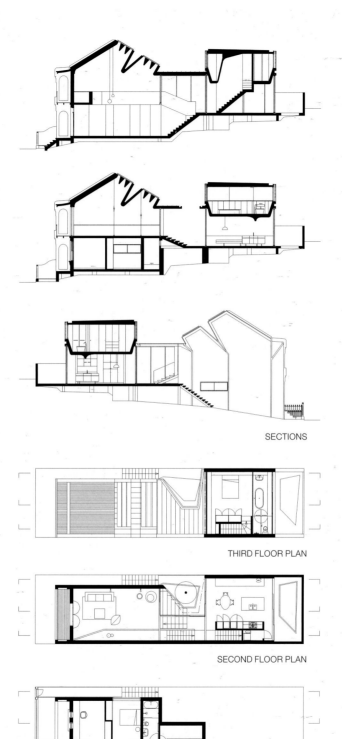

SECTIONS

THIRD FLOOR PLAN

SECOND FLOOR PLAN

FIRST FLOOR PLAN

Opposite: On the house's ground level, the living space and the kitchen/dining space are arranged around a central court-yard, which allows both access to natural light at either end.
Left: A view across the living room from the balcony along the front facade toward the interior courtyard.

Right: From the interior the telescoping skylight structures appear as a sculptural ceiling composed of a series of curves, folds, and gaps. Opposite: In the kitchen/dining space the ceiling still maintains a fluid, sculptural presence.

Contrasting the material palette of cast concrete structural elements and flooring and sculpted white plaster on the ceiling of the main living level, the upper master bedroom level (opposite) and lower guest bedroom level (left) feature rich gum wood cabinetry and wainscoting.

Architect Thomas Phifer transformed an apartment overlooking the Metropolitan Museum of Art into a remarkably open and airy residence for an art collector. Here, a view from the entrance vestibule toward the living room and Central Park beyond.

THOMAS PHIFER AND PARTNERS
FIFTH AVENUE APARTMENT
NEW YORK, NEW YORK

In addition to a host of prestigious cultural and educational commissions, architect Thomas Phifer has amassed an impressive portfolio of residential projects since establishing his firm in 1997, many in New York State's Hudson River Valley. Phifer cut his teeth with significant experience in the offices of Gwathmey Siegel and Associates and Richard Meier, themselves American modernist masters whose residential projects are experiments in the perfection of their distinctive styles, and Phifer's houses take on a similarly experimental aspect. They are the distillation of Phifer's rigorous and attenuated high modernist vocabulary in the service of a particularly refined and fearless coterie of clients. This apartment overlooking the Metropolitan Museum of Art in New York, however, represents Phifer's first foray into the redesign of a Manhattan apartment, and it is a remarkable translation of his design philosophy from country to city.

The original 1,500-square-foot apartment, in a classic Upper East Side residential building dating from 1929, was composed of a series of small rooms carved out of what was once a much larger apartment. Rather than maximizing the use of space, Phifer decided to maximize the impact of the space, creating an almost open-plan layout with one bedroom where once there had been two. The apartment's newly conceived openness not only replaces interior walls with copious natural light but also creates a showcase for the client's collection of Minimalist art and early-twentieth-century modernist furniture, including work by Donald Judd, Agnes Martin, Le Corbusier, and Jean Prouvé. To achieve the apartment's free-flowing, gallery-like spaces, Phifer distilled its spaces into two discrete zones: an open living, dining, and kitchen space, and a sleeping space. Secondary spaces include an entry vestibule, carefully concealed storage spaces, and a bathroom and powder room, both occupying cubic volumes partially composed of translucent glass.

Phifer echoed the client's collection by introducing a sculptural dimension to the apartment's organization, materials, and details. Each of the two main spaces contains a large freestanding cabinet made of maple plywood and maintaining a monumentality worthy of Minimalist sculpture. In addition to providing storage space, the cabinet in the main living space accommodates and conceals the kitchen cooktop; additional counter space and appliances are concealed within the adjacent wall behind sliding translucent panels. In the sleeping space the cabinet extends to function as a platform for the bed while also dividing the relatively large space to create a sitting area behind the bed. Perhaps the most sculptural elements introduced by Phifer are the deep, angular window surrounds, which are stainless steel polished to a mirrorlike sheen.

Right: Deep, angular window surrounds are stainless steel polished to a mirror-like sheen. Opposite, bottom: The living, dining, and kitchen spaces occupy a single, simple, large volume.

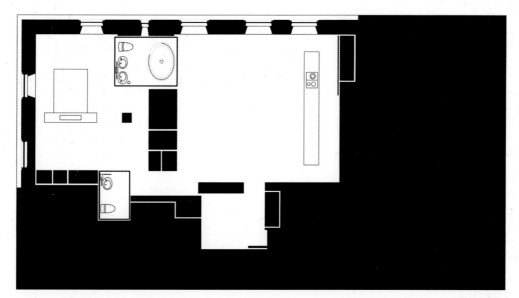

PLAN

The apartment's newly conceived openness serves as a showcase for the client's collection of Minimalist art and early-twentieth-century modernist furniture, including work by Donald Judd, Agnes Martin, Le Corbusier, and Jean Prouvé.

The freestanding maple plywood storage cabinets in the bedroom and main living space maintain a monumentality worthy of Minimalist sculpture. In the sleeping space the cabinet extends to function as a platform for the bed while also dividing the relatively large space to create a sitting area (opposite), while the cabinet in the main living space accommodates and conceals the kitchen cooktop (left).

245

Left: The master bathroom occupies what is essentially a translucent box and features sculptural fixtures that maintain a level of formal refinement that characterizes the entire apartment. Opposite: The concrete floor and mirror-polished stainless steel ceiling of the entry vestibule are a fitting introduction to the home of a collector of Minimalist art.

WELLS MACKERETH
LITTLE VENICE HOUSE
LONDON, UK

Out of a dormant commercial context, architect Sally Mackereth of Wells Mackereth has crafted a one-of-a-kind house that integrates industrial and antique details with modern domestic functions. The house is sited within the Little Venice section of London's tony Maida Vale, composed of streets lined with closely situated Victorian mansions, though its lot was previously occupied by a pair of nonresidential structures: a carriage house toward the front of the site, and a workshop toward the rear. Consistent with the mix-and-match nature of the project overall, Mackereth renovated the wood-framed carriage house and demolished the workshop, replacing it with an entirely new construction of austere zinc panels, brick, and plate glass.

The client desired a house with few rooms in favor of large spaces, which allowed Mackereth to develop an exceedingly simple organizational program for the project: bedroom suite in the front carriage house, and an open living, dining, and kitchen space in the new construction on the site of the old workshop. And while that sounds straightforward enough, the execution of this streamlined program in fact resulted in a richly variegated series of spaces rife with unexpected and delightful materials and details. Additionally, the soaring height of the new construction and the sharp-peaked eaves of the carriage house accommodate two discrete mezzanine levels, each with its own staircase. One of these, above the kitchen and overlooking the living and dining space, contains a study; the other, overlooking the bedroom, contains a decadent bathroom, with a freestanding tub on a platform perched over the bed like a canopy.

One of Mackereth's more charming touches is the threshold between the old and new structures, which takes the form of a large hidden doorway disguised as a bookcase—call it Hollywood Gothic, a term equally applicable to the wood panels and shutters in the bedroom, newly crafted to look positively antiquated. No less dramatic though thoroughly modern is the two-story-high pane of glass that pivots out from the main living space via a system of hydraulic pistons to form a temporary canopy over the adjacent outdoor terrace. Other mechanical flourishes appear throughout the house, including exposed unfinished steel beams and the systems of winches and cables that raise and lower a television screen and the chandelier over the dining table.

This house in London's Maida Vale designed by architect Sally Mackereth is composed of a pair of non-residential structures: a carriage house toward the front of the site, and a workshop, shown here, toward the rear.

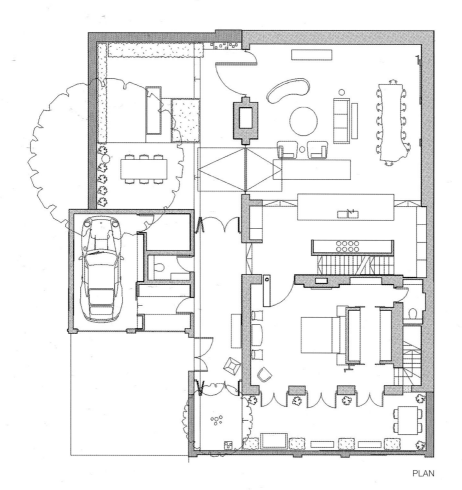

PLAN

Mackereth demolished the original workshop structure, replacing it with an entirely new construction of austere zinc panels, brick, and pivoting plate glass panes, one of which is two stories high and forms a temporary canopy over the adjacent outdoor terrace (top left and right).

The structure replacing
the original rear work-
shop building contains
a soaring, open living,
dining, and kitchen
space with dramatic
skylights, exposed steel
beams, and expanses
of brick.

Left: Hand cranks operate a system of winches and cables that raise and lower the chandelier over the dining room table. Opposite: Above the kitchen and overlooking the living and dining space, a mezzanine contains a study.

Opposite: Entry from
the main living area
to the master bedroom
is through a large
hidden doorway dis-
guised as a bookcase.
Left: Another hand-
cranked cable raises
and lowers the televi-
sion in the bedroom.

257

A second mezzanine level, in the master bedroom and accessible by way of its own staircase, accommodates the decadent master bath, perched over the bed like a canopy.

WORK ARCHITECTURE COMPANY
WHITE STREET LOFT
NEW YORK, NEW YORK

Architects Dan Wood and Amale Andraos of Work Architecture Company describe this residence for a family of four as an "inverse triplex," occupying as it does the full ground level and partial basement and sub-basement levels in a cast-iron warehouse building in lower Manhattan's TriBeCa neighborhood. Though the six-thousand-square-foot residence is composed in part of a series of spectacular, large-scaled spaces suited for entertaining, the architects' brief also included the provision of spaces for real-life family living, prompting a distinct division between public and private zones as well as a playful arrangement of smaller-scale spaces for family activities. Connecting all of these various functions and variously scaled spaces is a complex system of circulation incorporating multiple staircases, a ladder, a bridge, and variations in floor levels, giving the project a fun-house quality.

Entrance to the home directly accesses the living room, though the bourne seating surrounding a thin structural column signals that this particular living space belongs to the house's public realm. Two steps up lead to a spectacular transitional space in the form of a bamboo-lined box-like room that features a full bar and tables that mechanically rise from the floor for Japanese-style dining and that can function as a generously scaled dance floor when the tabletops are retracted. Beyond this space lie the semipublic family spaces, including the open kitchen and dining area, and beyond that the family room, which is lined in gray felt on the floor, ceiling, and walls, lending it a womblike sense of privacy and quiet. Here a ladder leads up to a sleeping loft, also lined in felt.

Two sets of stairs with sculptural plywood banisters lead up and down, respectively, to the most private zones of the house. The staircase leading up rises a half level to a floor devoted to the two children's bedrooms, each containing its own study space overlooking a series of light wells that bring natural illumination to the basement level, one floor below. That basement level contains the master bedroom suite, including a spacious office-gym and a wooden deck tucked under one of the light wells from the ground level. A staircase enclosed in translucent plastic bridges a gap between the his-and-her closets over the sub-basement level, which accommodates the nanny's bedroom, a large guest suite, a playroom with elevated stage, and a hermetic, hexagonal den sequestered away from the rest of this very sociable house like a genie's bottle.

This residence occupying 6,000 square feet over three levels in a cast-iron warehouse building in lower Manhattan's TriBeCa neighborhood is composed in part as a series of spectacular, large-scaled spaces suited for entertaining, such as this bamboo-lined room that can function as a dance floor.

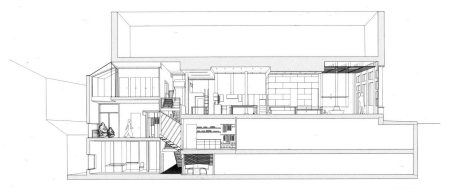

SECTION

FIRST FLOOR PLAN

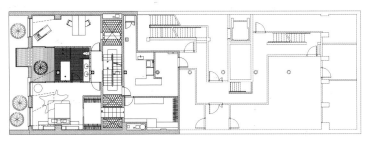

CELLAR PLAN

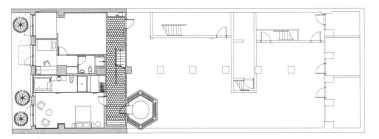

SUB-CELLAR PLAN

Entrance to the home
directly accesses the
living room (opposite,
top), which flows
into the transitional
bamboo-lined room
(opposite, bottom).

Right: In the residence's entrance cum living room, the space's public function is signaled by the bourne seating surrounding a thin structural column.
Opposite: The bamboo-lined room functions as a transitional space between the residence's most pubic realm at the front of the building and a semipublic realm composed of the kitchen, dining spaces, and family room.

The bamboo-lined room features tables that mechanically rise from the floor for Japanese-style dining.

The multilevel private
realm is situated at the
rear of the residence
behind a playfully com-
posed interior facade.

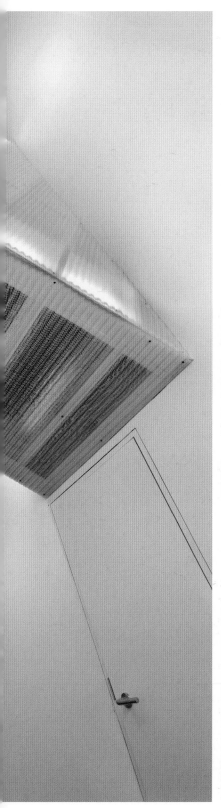

An intricate series of stairs, ladders, and even a bridge access the various components of the residence's private realm, including the ladder to the sleeping loft off the family room (far left), the ramp-like enclosed stair connecting the master bedroom and its closets (center), and the series of switchback stairs to the basement and sub-basement levels.

Right: The master bedroom (top) and guest suite (bottom) are serene oases within the home's high-energy composition. Opposite: The shared bath between the two children's rooms.

The rear facade is composed of a series of light wells that bring natural illumination to the basement level (bottom left). Each of the children's studies overlooks these light wells (top left), at the bottom of which is the basement-level deck off the master bedroom suite.

MESSANA O'RORKE
CHARLES STREET TOWNHOUSE
NEW YORK, NEW YORK

The width of this townhouse in Manhattan's West Village belies its relatively compact interior: the house's shallow depth yields a total square footage of 2,800 over four stories, including a full basement. When architects Brian Messana and Toby O'Rorke took on the task of renovating the historic house, which was originally constructed in 1853, they were confronted with a warren of small rooms that crowded all four floors. The architects' challenge, then, was to imbue the structure with a sense of openness and to create a spatial program that responded to contemporary living while respecting the integrity of the original structure, barely detectable as it was following a series of ill-conceived renovations. With the house granted landmark status, the architects' first move was the careful restoration of all elements on the street façade, including windows, brickwork, lintels, and railings.

Inside, the architects started from whole cloth, completely redistributing spaces on all four floors and cleansing the interior of the layers of extraneous details that accrued over the years. In addition to a shallow footprint, the house is distinguished by its wedge-shaped plan, an irregularity the architects addressed by installing elegant cabinet-like closets tucked into the angled east wall on all four floors. They thus created straightforward, squared-off rooms that are easily livable while introducing a variety of storage solutions to conceal not only clothing but all manner of media equipment and mechanical systems, allowing for a series of remarkably clean-lined interior spaces. This minimalist approach extends to the entire material palette: white walls stripped of moldings, with recessed lighting at their perimeter; honey-toned oak floors on the top three levels and matching wood composing the sculptural narrowly winding staircase (with sparely designed stainless-steel railings); dark limestone flooring on the basement level; attenuated, highly polished banisters; and marble fixtures and countertops in the bathrooms and kitchen.

The original structure of the Charles Street Townhouse dates from 1853, and the building's width belies the overall compactness of its footprint.

Entry to the house directly accesses the living room, which spans the full width of the first floor, and behind which are arranged a small study and a powder room on either side of the centrally placed staircase. On the basement level the dining room similarly extends along the entire width of the house, and service areas, i.e., kitchen and laundry/bathroom, are arrayed along the house's rear facade, an arrangement of service and served space that is applied to every level. The entire second floor is devoted to the master bedroom suite; and two bedrooms, each with its own bath, occupy the top floor, so that each floor of this idiosyncratic, many-lived house now enjoys a rational serenity.

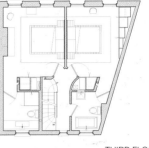

THIRD FLOOR PLAN

SECOND FLOOR PLAN

One enters the house immediately into the living room, which spans the building's full width. The staircase, a study, and a powder room, all compact, are tucked along the house's rear facade.

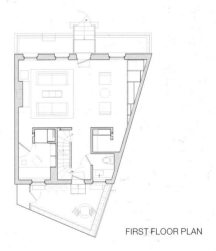

FIRST FLOOR PLAN

BASEMENT PLAN

On the basement level the dining room occupies the area immediately beneath the living room, with the rear zone of the floor occupied by the kitchen and another powder room.

Left: The sculptural, narrowly winding wooden staircase is complemented by sparely designed stainless-steel railings. Opposite: The generously proportioned master bedroom suite occupies the entire second floor.

Spectacular soaring spaces and copious natural light attracted architect Annabelle Selldorf to this project for the renovation of a unique loft space in a former YMCA in Chelsea.

ANNABELLE SELLDORF
CHELSEA LOFT
NEW YORK, NEW YORK

Architect Annabelle Selldorf's name is virtually synonymous with highly refined projects in the service of high culture—think of her exquisite renovation of the palatial beaux-arts mansion that is home to the Neue Galerie Museum for German and Austrian Art, on Manhattan's Upper East Side. So it is perhaps not a little ironic that this residential project for a family of three should have commissioned Selldorf to take on the renovation of a unique loft space in a former YMCA in Chelsea. Not only that, this unit, one of nine in the building, occupies part of what was once the gymnasium's running track and basketball court. But the loft's potential to offer spectacular soaring spaces and unending natural light serves as easy explanation for Selldorf's interest in the project.

The loft occupies 5,900 square feet on two levels, arrayed around a central double-height atrium space (particularly impressive in a duplex already composed of two high-ceilinged stories). Selldorf divided the raw space into two zones: public on the upper floor, and private on the lower. The upper level is composed of the open living, dining, and kitchen space as well as a guest bedroom and entry foyer/sitting room. To open up the spaces, Selldorf removed walls but retained a spectacularly long kitchen island, which she complemented with a custom-designed walnut table and built-in corner banquet that manages to offer accommodation for intimate family meals as well as for large dinner parties. One floor below, the lower level of the atrium functions as the family room. Around this are arranged the children's bedrooms and an expansive master bedroom suite that includes a remarkably spacious dressing room.

A large-scale metal staircase painted black with warm-toned wood treads connects the two levels in one of numerous gestures embracing the space's industrial structural elements and details. In this spirit industrial casement windows and black concrete floor tiles were introduced, and the massive trusses spanning the open spaces on the upper level were left exposed—a remarkable contrast with the warmth of the wood furniture scattered across the upper level and the colorful oversized sectional sofa designed by Gaetano Pesce in the lower-level atrium space. By virtue of such careful modulation of materials, color, and details, Selldorf managed to delineate within a cavernous blank canvas a series of spaces eminently suitable for family life.

UPPER LEVEL PLAN

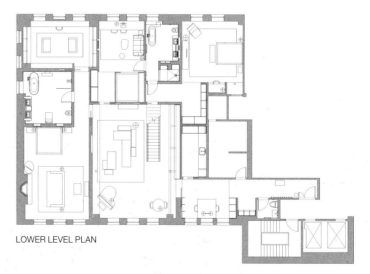

LOWER LEVEL PLAN

A colorful oversized
sectional sofa
designed by Gaetano
Pesce dominates
the lower level of the
double-height atrium,
which functions as
a family room.

The loft occupies what was once part of the former YMCA's running track, on the upper level, and basketball court, on the lower level.

Selldorf retained an existing long kitchen island (opposite), which she complemented with a custom-designed walnut table and built-in corner banquet that manages to offer accommodation for intimate family meals as well as for large dinner parties (left).

The pristine finishes and fixtures in the kitchen and the master bathroom are expressive of Selldorf's highly refined design approach.

On the loft's upper level, industrial casement windows, black concrete floor tiles, and the massive exposed trusses nicely contrast the warmth of the wood furniture.

ILLUSTRATION
CREDITS

HARRISON STREET RESIDENCE
MICHAEL MORAN/OTTO

VERTICAL HOUSE
JUERGEN NOGAI

SAN SEBASTIÁN APARTMENT
DEIDI VON SCHAEWEN

PITCH BLACK HOUSE
YOKO INOUE

BERESFORD APARTMENT
SCOTT FRANCES

BROOKLYN BROWNSTONE
PETER AARON/OTTO

EAST VILLAGE TOWNHOUSE
FRANCOIS HALARD/TRUNK ARCHIVE

WEINER TOWNHOUSE
COURTESY LOT-EK

FIFTH AVENUE APARTMENT, RICHARD MEIER
SCOTT FRANCES/OTTO

GHENT APARTMENT
PIETER-JAN DE PUE

BRICK WEAVE HOUSE
STEVE HALL © HEDRICH BLESSING

JACOBSEN RESIDENCE
COURTESY JACOBSEN ARCHITECTS

CRUSCH ALBA LOFT
BRUNO HELBLING, ZÜRICH

NYC LOFT
DEAN KAUFMAN

INVERTED WAREHOUSE/TOWNHOUSE
PAUL WARCHOL PHOTOGRAPHY

FLYNN MEWS HOUSE
COURTESY LORCAN O'HERLIHY ARCHITECTS

BLACK PEARL
FRANK HANSWIJK

FLOATING BUNGALOW
COURTESY BARBARA BESTOR ARCHITECTURE

ART COLLECTOR'S LOFT
IWAN BAAN

SKYLIGHT HOUSE
pp. 229–33, 235–37: JOHN GOLLINGS
p. 234: KATHERINE LU

FIFTH AVENUE APARTMENT, THOMAS PHIFER
AND PARTNERS
SCOTT FRANCES/OTTO

LITTLE VENICE HOUSE
RICHARD POWERS

WHITE STREET LOFT
ELIZABETH FELICELLA

CHARLES STREET TOWNHOUSE
ELIZABETH FELICELLA

CHELSEA LOFT
MANOLO YLLERA

ACKNOWLEDGMENTS

Thank you to the architects and photographers whose brilliant work fills these pages. My thanks also to Richard Meier for his thoughtful and elegant text. At Rizzoli International Publications I am grateful to publisher Charles Miers and associate publisher David Morton for their enthusiastic support, and to editor Alexandra Tart for her skill and patience. Special thanks go to graphic designer Claudia Brandenburg for the book's flawlessly executed layout. I would also like to thank Melanie Domino at 1100 Architect; Joel Sanders and Sam Hall at OTTO; Ian Dickenson at Lorcan O'Herlihy Architects; Sébastien Grandin at Studio Putman; Ama Ofeibea Amponsah and Michael Matey at Adjaye Associates; Nina Bransfield and Natalie Merelis at Ferguson & Shamamian Architects; Dan Terry at August; Lisa Green and Sara Martin at Selldorf Architects; Maureen Chung and Justin Stuart Rose at Trunk Archive; Marques McClary at LOT-EK; Edgar Almaguer at Richard Meier & Partners Architects; Chloe Hanson at John Pawson; Samantha Snodgrass at Studio Gang Architects; Lucas Blair Simpson and Jackie Furtado at Hedrich Blessing Photographers; Jan Kubasiewicz at Gus Wüstemann; John Patrick at Allied Works Architecture; Zachary Rousou at Dean/Wolf Architects; Claire de Zoete, Daphne Van Baardwijk, and Riekie Brokking at Zecc Architecten; Meara Daly at Neslon Daly Communications; Karen Murphy at UNStudio; Joshua Mulford at Chenchow Little; Stephen Varady at Thomas Phifer and Partners; Helen Bradbrook at Wells Mackereth Architects; and Jay Garfinkel at Work Architecture Company.